AA

SPOTTER
GUIDE

COASTAL

BIRDS

D0993330

© AA Media Limited 2011
Written by Lee Morgan

Produced for AA Publishing by D & N Publishing, Baydon, Wiltshire

Commissioning editor at AA Publishing: Paul Mitchell
Production at AA Publishing: Rachel Davis

Printed and bound in China by C&C Offset Printing Co. Ltd

A CIP catalogue record for this book is available from the British
Library.

ISBN 978 0 7495 6924 2
       978 0 7495 6928 0 (SS)

Published by AA Publishing, a trading name of AA Media Limited,
whose registered office is Fanum House, Basing View, Basingstoke,
Hampshire RG21 4EA. Registered number 06112600.

A04089
theAA.com/shop

CONTENTS

BIRDS ARE THE most popular and
conspicuous components of our
wildlife, and we all come across
them in everyday life. They tend to
be lively and vocal, many are large
and colourful and, as a group, they
are not so numerous that it is
difficult to get to know the
commoner species. In addition, their
mastery of the air remains a source
of wonder to humans.

DUNLIN, *the commonest wader around the British coast in winter.*

The *AA Spotter Guide to Coastal
Birds* covers the species of birds
most likely to be seen in England,
Scotland and Wales during a day trip to a local beach, and others that you
might see only on a visit to a remote island or nature reserve. Most are
common and widespread, not only on the coast but inland too, while
others are rare and have a restricted range, and some are migrant visitors
that may be found on our shores only at certain times of year. Naturally,
the book also includes many of our true seabirds as a special incentive to
readers to pay a visit to some of the spectacular seabird colonies that
grace our shores for short periods every year.

Each species is given a full page and the text is concise to pack as much
information as possible into the available space. The species account begins
with the common English name and is followed by the species' scientific
name. The subsequent text is divided into sections: **FACT FILE**, which
covers the species' size, habitat preferences, food and voice;
IDENTIFICATION, which describes its appearance; **STATUS AND HABITS**,
which describes where the species occurs (if a specific range is not given,
the species is widespread across Britain in suitable habitats), its population
status, and behavioural traits that assist with identification; **KEY FACT**,
which provides tips on unique information separating this species from
close relatives. The photographs are of adults unless indicated otherwise.

Birds are a group of vertebrates that are distinguished by having feathers, and that are generally able to fly. The ability to fly enables birds to exploit many habitats and sources of food, flee harsh weather, escape from predators, or display to other birds in the breeding season. The size and colour of different feather groups (called tracts) on a bird enable us to identify different species; examples of this are shown on the topography diagram.

After mating, female birds lay eggs in a nest, which can be an open construction of varied size and complexity, or a hole in a tree or building. The eggs are then incubated by either or both parents until the chicks hatch. Chicks of small birds and birds of prey tend to be fairly helpless and nest bound, entirely dependent on their parents for the first few days of life, whereas waterfowl chicks often leave the nest and are able to follow their parents within a day of hatching. They are taught by their parents how to find food.

Many birds are migratory, some travelling huge distances across the globe. Species that spend the northern temperate summer in Britain arrive from the warmer tropics to the south, returning there before the onset of winter. Our winter bird populations, meanwhile, are enhanced by the arrival of other species from further north and east.

SPOTTED REDSHANK, winter

crown
eye-stripe
supercilium
nape
upper mandible (bill)
mantle
scapulars
throat
lower mandible (bill)
primaries
breast
flank
tail
belly
undertail coverts

FINDING AND STUDYING COASTAL BIRDS

MANY COASTAL BIRDS are easy to find, as they live their lives alongside people, lingering around busy ports and harbours, on the rooftops of coastal towns, and even around noisy seaside funfairs. Many are highly adaptable and capable of exploiting a wide variety of habitats, even to the extent that they are now commonly seen around large reservoirs, rivers and lakes many kilometres inland.

A simple day at the beach can often provide great opportunities to get close views of some of our commonest coastal birds, but with practice it is possible to spot rarer species, too. Equally rewarding habitats are areas of clifftop scrub and among the tough grasses of windswept sand-dunes. Fishermen are often very familiar with some of the true 'seabirds' that live much of their lives out at sea, but spending time scanning the sea from an exposed coastal headland can provide views of species that few people ever see from the shore. Even a mundane ferry crossing can become an exciting adventure.

Springtime sees the arrival of migrant terns from the south, and sheer sea cliffs and remote islands bustle with the arrival of ocean-going seabirds returning to their colonies to breed. Summer is a busy season for nesting and rearing young, while the autumn brings visitors from the north, fleeing the onset of harsh conditions in the Arctic. Myriad geese, ducks and waders find Britain's relatively mild, ice-free conditions and sheltered sandy shores and saltmarshes the ideal location for the winter. So whatever the season, our varied coastal habitats attract a good variety of birds.

Coastal birds show a huge range of adaptations to their environment, with a great variety of bill shapes, leg lengths, feeding habits and migration patterns, all designed to cope with the diverse habitats in which they live. These habitats range from sheltered wooded undercliffs and long, shallow beaches of the south and east, to exposed rocky headlands of the north and west, carved by the pounding waves and surf of the Atlantic Ocean. Vast expanses of saltmarsh and muddy tidal estuaries, with shallow creeks and streams running across them, provide ideal feeding areas for migrating waders, and in winter they are often home to huge flocks of wildfowl. Dry coastal grasslands and shrubby coastal heaths offer food and shelter for tiny passerines; cliffs, boulder beaches and isolated islands provide nesting birds with refuge from hungry mammalian predators; and with every changing tide the sea exposes a rich and ever-changing supply of food. Man-made habitats are also of great importance – seafront buildings, piers, sea-walls, harbours and even buoys can all support different bird species.

It is easy to make your birdwatching purposeful, and for your sightings to help the conservation of birds and other wildlife. The British Trust for Ornithology (www.bto.org.uk) organises a range of surveys that rely on volunteers submitting records of the birds they have seen. You can take part in a survey of the birds that visit your garden, breeding birds of the wider countryside, and winter waterfowl of our coasts, estuaries and lakes. The Trust also has an online facility, called BirdTrack, which allows you to keep and access your observation records while contributing data on a local, national and international level. Conservation also relies on observers taking care not to interfere with breeding birds, and allowing flocks of winter visitors to get on with the business of feeding, preening and loafing without disturbance.

GLOSSARY

Cere Fleshy, waxy skin at the base of the upper bill, through which the nostrils open.

Eclipse The moulted plumage of ducks in summer, which for a short period renders them flightless; eclipse males resemble females.

Invertebrates All animals that lack a backbone, including insects.

Juvenile Young bird in its first year, but not yet in full adult plumage.

Lagoon Shallow body of water separated from the sea by a partial barrier of rock, sand, mud or gravel.

Lek Communal display ground.

Migration Mass regular movement of bird populations from one geographical region to another.

Pelagic Living in ocean waters away from land.

Primaries Strong, long flight feathers occupying the outer third and tip of the wing.

Saltmarsh Area of grassland and mud that is periodically inundated by salt water.

MUTE SWAN
Cygnus olor

FACT FILE

SIZE Length 145–160cm **HABITAT** Sheltered coasts and marshes, as well as a variety of freshwater habitats **FOOD** Plant material; sometimes small invertebrates **VOICE** Usually silent, but can make hissing sounds and coarse trumpeting

IDENTIFICATION

Adults have all-white plumage, although neck and head may be stained by muddy water. Large bill is orange-red with a large black knob at base, largest in male. Juveniles have buff-brown plumage and a dull pink bill, but moult into adult plumage in first winter. Neck is held in a graceful S-shape when swimming. Wings make whistling sounds in flight.

KEY FACT Male swans can be quite aggressive in the nesting season, fearlessly chasing off intruders with a great deal of hissing and wing-flapping. This 'busking' behaviour can be directed at humans as well as other swans.

MALE

LOCATION	DATE/TIME

STATUS AND HABITS

The commonest swan, and likely to be seen in a range of watery habitats, from sheltered coasts and tidal estuaries to city parks and lakes. Large weedy nests are built close to water, with both birds in attendance. Swans often feed by upending in deep water, using their long necks to reach food out of reach of other waterbirds. Large 'herds' of swans may gather in good feeding areas after the breeding season, and many move to the coast in winter.

FEMALE

BRENT GOOSE
Branta bernicla

FACT FILE

SIZE **Length 56–61cm** HABITAT **Large estuaries, saltmarshes, coastal grasslands** FOOD **Plant material: eelgrasses, seaweeds, grasses, saltmarsh plants** VOICE **Distinctive croaking *krrut*. Highly vocal, particularly when in large flocks**

IDENTIFICATION

Britain's smallest goose, uniformly dark and with a white rear end and black legs. Adults have a distinctive black head, neck and breast, with a band of white feathers on side of neck. Body colour varies according to subspecies: Pale-bellied shows a distinct margin between pale grey-buff belly, uniformly brownish back and black breast; Dark-bellied has no distinct margin between back and belly colour. Juveniles lack white neck band.

KEY FACT Brent Geese become quite tame towards the end of the winter. Close encounters with large flocks can afford observers the chance to distinguish between the two subspecies by carefully inspecting the body colours of individual birds.

LOCATION	DATE/TIME

STATUS AND HABITS

A winter visitor, appearing in large, noisy flocks in autumn. An estimated 100,000 birds migrate from their breeding grounds in the Arctic to the sheltered estuaries and saltmarshes of Britain and Ireland, where they graze in shallow water on eelgrasses and seaweeds, or on land in coastal marshes. Hungry flocks will often seek additional grazing in cultivated coastal pastures and farmland habitats during their stay. Typically, Pale-bellied Brents winter around the Irish coast, with some localised populations around the coast of Northumberland. The majority of Dark-bellied Brents spend the winter along the S and E coasts of England, especially N Norfolk and the Solent.

BARNACLE GOOSE
Branta leucopsis

FACT FILE

SIZE **Length 60–75cm** HABITAT **Marshes, mudflats, coastal pastures, arable fields** FOOD **Plant material: shoots, stems, leaves** VOICE **Short, staccato yapping, akin to the barking of a small dog**

IDENTIFICATION

A distinctively marked goose, appearing very black and white in flight. Adults have a creamy-white face that contrasts with black crown, neck and bill. Belly is pale grey-white, with subtle grey barring on flanks. Stern is white, and tail and legs are black. Back is slatey grey with black and white barring. Juveniles have a more blotchy appearance.

LOCATION	DATE/TIME

STATUS AND HABITS

A winter visitor to the region, with approximately **60,000** arriving on traditional sites each year from Oct. Birds that breed in Greenland tend to winter around the islands of NW Scotland (particularly Islay) and NW Ireland, while those that breed in Svalbard congregate around the Solway Firth. The Barnacle Goose is a predominantly coastal species and rarely found inland, although large flocks are frequently found grazing on a variety of coastal pastures and on arable farmland close to the sea.

KEY FACT

Barnacle Geese are commonly kept in captivity, the result being that feral birds frequently turn up in a variety of habitats throughout Britain, usually mixed in with flocks of other ducks and geese.

SHELDUCK
Tadorna tadorna

FACT FILE

SIZE **Length 60–70cm** HABITAT **Coastal marshes, muddy shores, inland gravel pits and lakes** FOOD **Small molluscs and crustaceans** VOICE **Male whistles; female quacks**

IDENTIFICATION
Bright red bill and pinkish legs of adults contrast with glossy, dark green head and neck and pale plumage. Has a dark orange chest-band and dark bands along wings. Sexes are alike but male is larger and has a large knob at base of bill. Juveniles are more mottled, with a dull pink bill.

KEY FACT Nests are built in deep cover, under dense bushes and even in old Rabbit holes. Females defend their young aggressively, and take them to the water soon after they hatch.

MALE

LOCATION	DATE/TIME

MALES

STATUS AND HABITS

Although most Shelducks live along coasts, the species has spread inland where there are gravel pits, large lakes and rivers with muddy margins. They feed by sweeping the bill from side to side over mud to sieve out tiny molluscs or shrimps; the margins of the bill have comb-like edges that act as filters. After the breeding season, large numbers of Shelducks gather at traditional sites on coastal marshes to moult their flight feathers, before dispersing again in winter.

MALLARD
Anas platyrhynchos

SIZE Length 50–65cm **HABITAT** Wide range of
wetland and coastal habitats, including urban sites
FOOD Wide range of plant and animal foods, scraps
VOICE Males have weak nasal calls; females quack

IDENTIFICATION

Male has mostly grey-brown plumage, but head is glossy green with a
yellow bill, and breast is chestnut below white collar. When dabbling, black
stern and white tail show clearly. Moulting males in summer are similar to
female, which is mostly mottled brown with a darker bill. In flight, both
sexes show a white-edged blue speculum. Juveniles resemble female.

KEY FACT This is one of our most abundant wildfowl species
with up to 350,000 pairs breeding in Britain each year, and many more
arriving in the winter from colder N regions.

MALE

LOCATION	DATE/TIME

STATUS AND HABITS

A common, widespread and familiar bird, in habitats ranging from sheltered coasts and marshes to city parks and inland lakes. Often very confident around people, readily taking food scraps and becoming very tame, but when nesting the females are extremely secretive, concealing their nests in deep vegetation, often away from the water. Large numbers of birds appear on the coast in winter when freezing weather conditions can drive them from freshwater ponds and lakes.

FEMALE

WIGEON
Anas penelope

SIZE Length 45–51cm **HABITAT** Breeds on lakes; winters on coastal grasslands and estuaries **FOOD** Plant leaves and shoots, especially eelgrasses and algae **VOICE** Males have shrill *whee-ooo* calls; females make quiet churring sounds

IDENTIFICATION
An attractive dabbling duck with a colourful appearance in good light. Male has an orange head with a yellow crown, and a pink-tinged breast. Most of the plumage is grey above, but underside is white and stern black. Female is mostly brown with a white belly and dull orange flanks. In flight, female's wings look dark, but male's show large white patches. Juveniles resemble female.

KEY FACT The wintering population of Wigeon in Britain greatly exceeds the summer breeding population, as many thousands of birds from Iceland and N Scandinavia head for our ice-free estuaries and coastal marshes.

MALE

LOCATION	DATE/TIME

STATUS AND HABITS

In the breeding season **Wigeons** are very shy, and are confined mainly to remote **N** areas such as upland lakes and peat bogs, where they live fairly solitary lives. In winter, however, they all head for the coast, especially large estuaries where they can feed on algae as the tide retreats. At high tide they move to nearby coastal grasslands and marshes in conspicuous and noisy flocks that sometimes take off together, calling loudly.

FEMALE

TEAL
Anas crecca

SIZE Length 34–38cm HABITAT Shallow lakes and ponds in summer; sheltered estuaries and coastal marshes in winter FOOD Invertebrates, seeds VOICE Chirping, high-pitched *krick*

IDENTIFICATION

The smallest duck of the region, with a compact shape and distinctive plumage. Male has an orange-brown head with a large, yellow-edged green patch over eye running back to nape. Back and flanks are mostly grey and underparts are white. Rear view shows a black stern with creamy-yellow side patches. Female and juveniles are similar, with grey-brown plumage. All show a green speculum and white underwing in flight.

KEY FACT Most Teals that breed in N Europe head SW in winter, mainly to Britain's coasts, although some travel even further – often as far S as North Africa. All migrate N again in spring.

MALE

LOCATION	DATE/TIME

STATUS AND HABITS

A widespread and, in some places, very common duck, present all year in Britain, but very secretive in the breeding season. When alarmed, Teals take off vertically with rapid wingbeats and a swerving flight, soon dropping into cover again. Flocks often fly in formation, resembling waders. They prefer to feed in shallow water, sifting soft mud with side-to-side bill movements. Huge flocks congregate in winter after leaving their **N** breeding grounds, but hunting pressure makes them very wary of humans.

FEMALE

GREATER SCAUP
Aythya marila

FACT FILE

SIZE **Length 42–51cm** HABITAT **Winter visitor to coasts and estuaries** FOOD **Mainly aquatic molluscs** VOICE **Usually silent, but makes harsh, grating calls in flight**

IDENTIFICATION

At a glance, male **Greater Scaup** is similar to male **Tufted Duck**, but back is grey, and head shows a dark green gloss and lacks a crest. Female has mostly brown plumage with a darker head, yellow eye and large, pale patches at base of bill, forehead and cheeks. In flight, both sexes show conspicuous white wingbars. Juveniles resemble female.

KEY FACT Coastal flocks in winter consist of adults and juveniles, which keep together in family groups. Young males start to moult into adult plumage by the end of their first winter, but do not gain full adult plumage until their second winter.

MALE

LOCATION	DATE/TIME

STATUS AND HABITS

The Greater Scaup is a winter visitor to Britain from its coastal tundra breeding grounds in Scandinavia and Iceland, arriving on our coasts in autumn when driven SW by harsh weather. Its preferred habitat is shallow coastal lagoons and bays where it can dive for small molluscs. When not feeding, flocks remain on the water, bobbing in the waves, often sleeping like this until the tide drops. Occasional birds turn up on inland lakes and gravel pits, but they are unlikely to find sufficient food in fresh waters.

FEMALE

EIDER
Somateria mollissima

SIZE **Length 50–70cm** HABITAT **Estuaries to rocky shores; almost exclusively coastal** FOOD **Shellfish (especially mussels), crustaceans** VOICE **Male produces an unmistakable cooing *ah-ooo***

IDENTIFICATION

A bulky duck with a distinctive sloping forehead that runs straight in line with the wedge-shaped bill. Apart from during the summer moult, the sexes look markedly different. Male is strikingly black and white, with a black crown, underparts and tail contrasting with white upperparts, lime-green nape and pinkish breast. Female has a uniformly brown body with dark barring, affording good camouflage when nesting. Juveniles resemble female, but are duller grey-brown with more diffuse markings.

KEY FACT

Eider nests are insulated with feathers that the female carefully plucks from her own breast. This eiderdown, famous for its softness and warmth, is harvested from the nests when they are abandoned and used to stuff pillows and quilts.

MALE

LOCATION	DATE/TIME

STATUS AND HABITS

These highly gregarious birds can be seen throughout the year around the coasts of Scotland, NE England and N Ireland. More than 30,000 pairs of birds breed here, the males courting the females by cooing and throwing their heads backwards. Winter populations are bolstered by tens of thousands of migrant birds and the range extends to the coast of S England. Eiders are a true seaduck and will dive for food in the roughest conditions, often close to the beach or just beyond the breaking surf.

FEMALE

COMMON SCOTER
Melanitta nigra

FACT FILE

SIZE **Length 44–54cm** HABITAT **A few pairs breed
on N lakes in summer; exclusively coastal but mostly offshore
in winter** FOOD **Molluscs** VOICE **Male produces a coarse piping
during courtship**

IDENTIFICATION

A small, uniformly dark seaduck. Male is totally black (sometimes with a
subtle iridescent sheen on head) with a prominent bright yellow ridge
(culmen) on the bulbous black bill. Female and juveniles are generally
very dark brown with pale buff cheeks.

KEY FACT In winter, dense flocks of Common Scoters
congregate in favoured areas along the Moray Firth, Carmarthen and
Cardigan bays, and the N Norfolk coast. It is rare to find solitary birds.

MALE

LOCATION	DATE/TIME

STATUS AND HABITS

Common Scoters are highly gregarious ducks, often seen flying in long, trailing lines low over the sea or congregating in large rafts, sometimes of several hundred birds, on the open ocean. Adult birds will dive up to 30m to hunt for molluscs, and frequently favour feeding in areas of deep water with a sandy seabed. Most birds seen in the winter are Scandinavian migrants. Breeding birds in our region favour small lochs in N and W Scotland, where they nest in dense waterside vegetation.

FEMALE

VELVET SCOTER
Melanitta fusca

FACT FILE

SIZE Length 51–58cm HABITAT Winter visitor only,
mostly offshore FOOD Invertebrates, small fish, some
plant material VOICE Usually silent; males display call
is a repeated *chuc-chuc-chuc*, followed by gurgling

IDENTIFICATION

Both sexes are larger and stockier than the Common Scoter, with a
longer bill and white patches on rear of wing (more obvious in flight).
Male is black with a white 'teardrop' eye mark and yellow-sided bill.
Female is sooty brown with two pale patches on face, one on cheek and
one at base of bill. Juvenile resembles female but has a paler belly and
whiter facial markings.

KEY FACT It is estimated that approximately 3,000 Velvet
Scoters migrate to Britain's coastline every winter. Occasionally, stray
birds turn up on large inland lakes and reservoirs.

MALE

LOCATION	DATE/TIME

STATUS AND HABITS

Velvet Scoter is a non-breeding winter visitor from its nesting grounds in Scandinavia. Generally appearing on the E coast of Scotland and England in autumn, its wintering range can extend as far S as the NE Mediterranean. Small flocks are often loosely associated with larger flocks of Common Scoter, but larger flocks of wintering Velvet Scoter are sometimes found along the sheltered coasts of NE Scotland, particularly in the Moray Firth. The ducks dive frequently for food and generally favour feeding over deep water with a sandy seabed.

FEMALE

GOLDENEYE
Bucephala clangula

FACT FILE

SIZE Length 42–50cm **HABITAT** Nests near forested lakes in the N; winters on sheltered coasts and large lakes **FOOD** Aquatic invertebrates **VOICE** Mostly silent, but may give croaking display calls

IDENTIFICATION

A compact diving duck with distinctive 'peaked' head outline. Male's head is dark glossy green with a white patch on face and a yellow eye. Body is mostly white with a dark back and stern. Female's head is reddish brown, bill is grey with a pink patch near tip, and rest of plumage is greyish brown, paler on underside. Juveniles resemble female but with a dark eye.

KEY FACT Nests are often built in tree-holes near N lakes; birds also take readily to nestboxes, despite their extreme wariness of humans. Although they are diving ducks, they can perch in trees.

MALE

LOCATION	DATE/TIME

STATUS AND HABITS

The Goldeneye is most familiar as a winter visitor to Britain from its NE breeding grounds, when small flocks can be seen bobbing buoyantly in open water and diving frequently to feed. Birds favour ice-free water bodies, spending most time in fresh water but moving to the coast in very cold conditions, when they may gather in bays and estuaries. In early spring, males make their head-tossing displays, and pairs migrate N earlier than other ducks for the breeding season.

FEMALE

RED-BREASTED MERGANSER
Mergus serrator

FACT FILE

SIZE Length 52–58cm HABITAT Breeds on upland lakes and rivers; winters on sheltered coasts, harbours and estuaries FOOD Fish, some aquatic invertebrates VOICE Usually silent, may make quiet grating sounds

IDENTIFICATION

A slim, long-bodied duck with a long sawbill. Male has a red bill, legs and eyes, a glossy dark green head with an untidy crest, a white neck collar and a speckled brown breast. Upperparts are black and white, and flanks and underside are grey with fine markings. Female has grey-brown plumage and an orange head, also with an untidy crest. In flight, wings show large white patches. Juveniles resemble female.

KEY FACT The serrated bill is the perfect adaptation for capturing and holding onto slippery fish; Red-breasted Mergansers are good swimmers and can pursue small fish in fast-flowing rivers or the sea, sometimes bringing them to the surface before swallowing them.

MALE

LOCATION	DATE/TIME

STATUS AND HABITS

In summer, Red-breasted Mergansers are secretive birds, nesting
alongside clear lakes and rivers in the far **N** of Britain, Ireland, Iceland
and Scandinavia. In autumn, they migrate **S** to coasts, where they feed in
sheltered bays and estuaries, sometimes venturing inland to fresh waters.
By the end of the winter they start courtship, with males displaying to
groups of females. In areas with plenty of fish they may be present in
small flocks, but are less gregarious in summer.

FEMALE

LONG-TAILED DUCK
Clangula hyemalis

SIZE Length 40–55cm **HABITAT** Winter visitor to gently shelving coastal waters and open sea **FOOD** Molluscs, crustaceans, small fish **VOICE** Males utter a nasal *ow-ow-owalee*; females make a gentle quack

IDENTIFICATION
These small, neat ducks have pale bellies and dark wings. Sexes are dissimilar and colours highly variable; only male has long tail feathers and a pink band on bill. Winter male (the only plumage seen in Britain) is generally black and white with a buff face patch, turning brown, black and white in eclipse. Winter female is mostly brown and white, with a varying extent of white on face. Juveniles resemble autumn female but are more uniformly brown on face.

MALE

LOCATION	DATE/TIME

STATUS AND HABITS

A winter visitor to the region from its breeding grounds in Iceland and Norway. Over 10,000 birds arrive in Britain every winter, usually between Dec and Mar. They are highly gregarious and can form sizeable flocks, and are common off the sandy beaches of NE Scotland, Orkney and Shetland. They dive frequently in search of a variety of aquatic invertebrates, but while they feed in relatively shallow water they are rarely seen close to shore.

KEY FACT

Despite their small size and elegant plumage, Long-tailed Ducks are hardy seafarers and are able to remain at sea in even the roughest conditions.

FEMALE

GREAT NORTHERN DIVER
Gavia immer

FACT FILE

SIZE **Length 75–90cm** HABITAT **Winter visitor to open seas and rocky headlands; rarely stays in summer** FOOD **Fish, crustaceans** VOICE **Distinctive wailing song (seldom heard in region)**

IDENTIFICATION

A large, robust bird with a dagger-like bill. Head is held outstretched in flight, with feet and legs trailing behind. Winter adults have sooty grey-brown upperparts, a whitish throat, neck and underparts, and a grey bill. Summer adults have a silky black head and neck, with distinctive rows of white stripes on neck. Underparts are white, and upperparts are black with a chequerboard of spots. Juveniles resemble winter adults.

> **KEY FACT**   In North America the species is commonly known as the Loon. This is thought to refer to the bird's clumsy gait when on land, and may have its origins in the Icelandic word *luen*, meaning 'lame'.

SUMMER

LOCATION	DATE/TIME

STATUS AND HABITS

A non-breeding winter visitor (the majority of birds seen in the region breed on large lakes in Iceland). Outside of the breeding season adult birds are generally solitary, occasionally seen in loose groups of twos and threes. They are able to withstand rough sea conditions and are commonly seen fishing off exposed rocky headlands, where they dive frequently in search of fish, crabs and other marine invertebrates. Occasionally, non-breeding adults will remain in the region throughout the summer.

JUVENILE

RED-THROATED DIVER
Gavia stellata

FACT FILE

SIZE Length 55–65cm HABITAT Breeds beside small moorland pools; winters in shallow coastal waters
FOOD Predominantly fish VOICE Guttural *gaa-gaa-gaa* in flight; plaintive *whaooo* around breeding areas

IDENTIFICATION

A small, elegant diver with an acutely upswept lower mandible on the sharp bill. Breeding adults have a blue-grey face and neck, black and white stripes on back of neck, and a red throat patch. Body is grey-brown with whitish underparts. Winter adults have grey upperparts covered with small white spots, and a bright white face and neck. Juveniles resemble winter adults.

KEY FACT   The Red-throated Diver swims with its head tilted upwards, which accentuates the apparent curvature of the bill. This makes it easy to distinguish from other divers, even at a great distance.

SUMMER

LOCATION	DATE/TIME

STATUS AND HABITS

The majority of the resident breeding population of about 1,000 pairs is confined to isolated moorland pools in N Scotland, with the main strongholds present on Shetland, Orkney and the Outer Hebrides. In winter, the widespread coastal populations are bolstered by birds from N Europe. Wintering birds are generally more numerous along the E coast of England and Scotland, where they dive in shallow open water in search of small fish.

WINTER

BLACK-THROATED DIVER
Gavia arctica

SIZE Length 60–70cm **HABITAT** Breeds on large lochs; winters mainly in shallow coastal waters **FOOD** Fish **VOICE** Distinctive wailing call and guttural croaking, mainly around breeding territories

IDENTIFICATION

Between the Red-throated and Great Northern divers in both size and appearance. Summer adults sport a grey head and nape, with a black throat patch bordered by black and white stripes. Upper body is black with a chequerboard of white spots. Underparts are pale. Winter adults have uniformly grey-black upperparts and whitish underparts, often with a distinctive white flash on flanks. Juveniles resemble winter adults.

KEY FACT

Black-throated Divers are easily disturbed at the nest and are highly vulnerable to marine pollution, making them a species of conservation concern.

SUMMER

LOCATION	DATE/TIME

STATUS AND HABITS

A rare and protected breeding bird that nests beside large lochs in the
Scottish Highlands – about 100 pairs breed in the region. Outside of the
breeding season, birds are predominantly coastal. The winter population is
greatly increased by an influx of birds from Scandinavia, with the E coasts
of Scotland and England providing the best opportunities for viewing at this
time. Birds appear buoyant in the water and dive frequently when fishing.
The dives are generally shallow (usually less than 6m) and last less than
a minute.

WINTER

RED-NECKED GREBE
Podiceps grisegena

FACT FILE

SIZE Length 40–45cm HABITAT Winter visitor to sheltered coasts and estuaries FOOD Invertebrates (particularly aquatic insects), small fish VOICE Harsh, rasping bray when breeding, otherwise silent in region

IDENTIFICATION

A stocky grebe with a distinctive yellow base to bill. Summer adults display a chestnut-red neck and breast, black cap and whitish cheeks. Upperparts are greyish brown, underparts are pale, and flanks have grey streaking. Winter adults are much duller and have a paler throat, but retain a hint of red on collar. Juveniles resemble winter adults but have more red on neck.

KEY FACT During long stretches of cold weather individuals will occasionally make flights to forage on larger lakes and reservoirs, providing observers the prospect of closer views.

SUMMER

LOCATION	DATE/TIME

STATUS AND HABITS

Most commonly encountered as a scarce winter visitor to the coastlines
of S and E Britain, although occasionally present year-round. Breeding
is suspected in Britain but considered very rare. European birds
breed on densely vegetated lakes inland. Usually 100 or so individuals
visit Britain between Oct and Mar, mostly feeding in shallow coastal
waters in large, sheltered bays and estuary mouths. They can be tricky
to spot in rough weather, and frequent periods of diving can make
prolonged observation difficult.

WINTER

LITTLE GREBE
Tachybaptus ruficollis

FACT FILE

SIZE **Length 25–29cm** HABITAT **Breeds on ponds, reedbeds and lagoon margins; winters in harbours, sheltered bays, estuaries** FOOD **Small fish, aquatic invertebrates** VOICE **High-pitched whinny; short, shrill calls**

IDENTIFICATION

The smallest grebe, with a compact body shape and a powderpuff tail, this often fluffed up. In clear water, the yellow-green legs and lobed feet show up. Male has a dark cap and chestnut nape in breeding season, with a green patch at base of bill. Female is more uniform brown but with a paler neck. Newly hatched young have striped plumage.

KEY FACT Most Little Grebes are sedentary, but in winter British local birds may be joined by many others from E Europe, which head W to escape freezing conditions. Ice-free water bodies are essential to their survival.

SUMMER

LOCATION	DATE/TIME

STATUS AND HABITS

Resident throughout the year in suitable water bodies, Little Grebes can be found across most of Britain and Ireland, with some birds moving to larger lakes or sheltered coasts in freezing conditions. Excellent swimmers, with the legs set well back on the body, but rarely seen on dry land as they are unable to walk easily. Excellent buoyancy enables them to spend most of their time on the water, preening and sleeping as well as feeding. Floating weedy nests are built at the water's edge.

WINTER

GREAT CRESTED GREBE
Podiceps cristatus

FACT FILE

SIZE Length 46–51cm HABITAT Breeds on ponds, lakes and lochs with weedy margins; winters on sheltered coasts, large harbours, estuaries FOOD Mainly fish, but also some aquatic invertebrates VOICE Usually silent; harsh staccato notes in spring

IDENTIFICATION

A streamlined waterbird with a slender neck and long, pointed bill. Adults look mainly black and white from a distance, but closer views show a grey-brown back, white flanks, a dark cap and a pink bill. In spring, conspicuous orange, chestnut-brown and black ear tufts develop. Winter plumage is more uniform pale grey-brown. Newly hatched young are fluffy, and striped black and white.

LOCATION	DATE/TIME

> **KEY FACT**
>
> The species' spectacular courtship display includes head-shaking with the ear tufts and crest spread out, and the 'penguin dance'. Ritual preening and offerings of billfuls of water plants are also part of the display.

STATUS AND HABITS

Great Crested Grebes occur across a wide range of watery habitats, as long as there is a plentiful supply of fish and suitable safe nest sites. Floating weedy nests are fixed amongst marginal plants and the newly hatched young are tended by both parents, often taking rides on their backs. Excellent swimmers, they are able to pursue quite large fish underwater, and only leave an area if freezing conditions prevent diving for food; they are then likely to be found on sheltered coasts.

JUVENILE

SLAVONIAN GREBE
Podiceps auritus

FACT FILE

SIZE **Length 31–38cm** HABITAT **Breeds on weedy pools and lakes; winters on sheltered coasts** FOOD **Fish** VOICE **Various high-pitched calls in spring, otherwise silent**

IDENTIFICATION

A striking bird in its breeding plumage, with rich brick-red flanks, a black back and head, and conspicuous bright orange ear tufts stretching back from red eye. Black bill has a white tip. Winter adults have mostly pale grey plumage with a black cap, black down back of neck, white underside and red eye. Juveniles resemble winter adults but with dusky cheeks.

KEY FACT A few pairs of Slavonian Grebes nest in secret locations in Scotland, but the bulk of the population nests in Iceland, Scandinavia and N Europe, and then migrates S and W to coastal areas for the winter.

SUMMER

LOCATION	DATE/TIME

STATUS AND HABITS

The species' showy courtship display may be seen at breeding sites, when birds rush at each other on the water with bills filled with water weeds. Floating weedy nests are constructed on lake margins, where birds may nest colonially. This species is most familiar as a winter visitor to Britain, where it may be seen on sheltered coasts, sometimes in loose mixed flocks with other grebes. Even in rough seas Slavonian Grebes remain on the water, becoming difficult to spot because of their frequent dives.

WINTER

FULMAR
Fulmarus glacialis

FACT FILE

SIZE **Wingspan 100–115cm** HABITAT **Coastal and pelagic; nests on sea cliffs** FOOD **Fish, squid, crustaceans, carrion** VOICE **Various guttural chuckles are uttered around nest**

IDENTIFICATION

A stocky, gull-like relative of petrels and shearwaters, reminiscent of a small albatross, and with characteristic tube nostrils. Adults have a white head, underparts and tail, with a subtle grey smudge around eye. Upperparts and back are uniformly grey. Easily recognisable in flight thanks to its stiff wings, shallow wingbeats, and effortless banking and gliding.

KEY FACT Until the end of the 19th century, breeding Fulmars were found only on the remote island of St Kilda. They now breed in any suitable habitats around the entire coastline of the British Isles.

LOCATION	DATE/TIME

STATUS AND HABITS

Common around all British coastlines but generally more numerous further N. Nest on ledges and sea cliffs. Nesting birds are capable of regurgitating the oily (and smelly) contents of their crop as a defence against nest predators. Birds are usually present year-round in the vicinity of breeding areas, but adults generally move offshore after the breeding season (Mar–Aug). Effective opportunistic ocean scavengers, Fulmars are frequently first on the scene when dead fish and fish offal are being discarded by fishing boats.

MANX SHEARWATER
Puffinus puffinus

FACT FILE

SIZE **Wingspan 70–85cm** HABITAT **Pelagic; breeds in burrows on islands** FOOD **Fish, squid, small crustaceans** VOICE **Silent at sea; strangled cooing and coughing call at breeding sites**

IDENTIFICATION

A small shearwater with a long, thin bill and small tube nostrils. Uniformly black upperparts contrast with predominantly white underparts, apart from black margin to underwing. Very characteristic are the long, straight wings and stiff-winged flight, often low over the water, with frequent banking and 'shearing'.

STATUS AND HABITS

A very common bird in the region, but a highly pelagic species that spends much of its life out at sea. Birds can be seen, sometimes in large numbers, from exposed headlands along the W coast. They skim the water with a characteristic 'shearing' flight, and feeding flocks will sometimes form dense 'rafts' on the surface. Manx Shearwaters come to land only to breed, between May and Sep. Breeding birds nest in burrows on remote islands, feeding at sea by day and returning to the nest after dark.

LOCATION	DATE/TIME

KEY FACT

Manx Shearwaters have a very long lifespan – individuals over 55 years old have been recorded in Britain.

STORM-PETREL
Hydrobates pelagicus

FACT FILE

SIZE Length 14–16cm HABITAT Pelagic; breeds in crevices and burrows on remote islands FOOD Surface plankton, small fish, crustaceans VOICE Silent at sea; strange guttural purring when breeding

KEY FACT Seawatching from exposed headlands on the W coast can provide the best viewing opportunities, particularly from Aug to Sep, when NW gales can force migrating birds closer to the shore.

IDENTIFICATION

A tiny seabird, only a little larger than a sparrow, with a characteristic fluttering flight low over the water. Adults have a uniformly dark sooty-brown (appearing black at distance) head and body, and a bright white rump. In flight, birds show a square-ended tail and white bar on underwing. Juveniles resemble adults but may show a pale wingbar on upperwing.

LOCATION	DATE/TIME

STATUS AND HABITS

Upwards of 100,000 pairs may breed in the region, but the species is highly pelagic and rarely seen close to shore. Birds come to shore only to breed, typically at night. They nest in rock crevices, drystone walls and burrows on remote offshore islands, where mammalian predators are absent. Despite their small size, Storm-petrels are hardy ocean wanderers, seemingly unaffected by stormy seas and high winds. Feeding birds flutter low over the water with their feet dangling and wings held high in a distinctive 'V'.

CORMORANT
Phalacrocorax carbo

IDENTIFICATION

A large waterbird with a bulky body, short, strong legs and feet, broad wings and a powerful bill with a hooked tip. Adult plumage is mostly dark with a scaly appearance and a green gloss in breeding season. White thigh patches develop in early spring, chin is white and bill has a yellow base. Juveniles are much browner, with extensive areas of white on underside.

KEY FACT After a session in the water, Cormorants can be seen rubbing their bill on the base of their tail to obtain oil from the preen gland, before meticulously preening each feather to maintain waterproofing.

LOCATION	DATE/TIME

STATUS AND HABITS

Cormorants are powerful birds, able to swim well in pursuit of fish on the seabed, and are often seen emerging at the surface with a wriggling eel or Flounder. After a fishing session they are often seen perching near the water with wings outstretched. Despite having webbed feet they are able to perch in trees, where they sometimes nest, but cliffs are their favoured sites, and they may form large colonies. Cormorants are increasingly frequent on inland waterbodies like reservoirs, sometimes roosting on pylons.

SHAG
Phalacrocorax aristotelis

SIZE Length 65–85cm **HABITAT** Exclusively marine, favouring rocky coasts **FOOD** Fish **VOICE** Vocal around breeding colonies, producing harsh, coughing grunts; otherwise silent

IDENTIFICATION

Similar to the Cormorant but noticeably smaller and slimmer, and with a more slender bill that has a hooked tip. Breeding adults develop

a distinctive recurved crest, a bright yellow base to bill and a glossy green sheen over dark body. Winter adults lose crest and colours fade. Juveniles tend to be browner, with a pale throat.

STATUS AND HABITS

A common breeding bird, resident on rocky shorelines throughout the region but generally more abundant on N and W coasts. Shags are exclusively marine and are rarely found inland, nesting in colonies on sea-cliff ledges. Adult birds rarely venture very far from the nesting colony in the breeding season but generally remain at sea during the winter; they are tolerant of very rough sea conditions. They swim low in the water and dive frequently for fish, typically commencing dives with a forward 'leap' to propel themselves down into the water.

LOCATION	DATE/TIME

KEY FACT

Over half of the region's 27,000 pairs of breeding birds are concentrated around less than 10 key sites, but the species is easy to see around most large seabird colonies.

GANNET
Morus bassanus

FACT FILE

SIZE Wingspan 170–190cm HABITAT Pelagic and
coastal seas; nests on inaccessible cliffs FOOD Fish (predominantly
pelagic shoaling species) VOICE Harsh gargling around breeding areas

IDENTIFICATION

A very large and distinctive seabird in flight, with very long, pointed wings,
a cigar-shaped body and a large dagger-like bill. Adults are predominantly
white, with a yellow-buff head and black wingtips. Juveniles are generally
brown, speckled with varying degrees of white according to age; it takes
five years for them to moult into full adult plumage.

LOCATION	DATE/TIME

KEY FACT

When hunting, Gannets can dive from heights of up to 30m, sometimes hitting the water at over 100kph! Their heads are filled with a complex network of air sacs that cushion their brain against the impact.

STATUS AND HABITS

A common seabird off Britain's coasts, often seen plunge-diving for fish from a great height. Britain and Ireland harbour over 200,000 breeding pairs (three-quarters of the world's population) in just 12 major colonies, these located on isolated islands and steep, inaccessible cliffs. Outside of the breeding season, most birds become exclusively pelagic, following the movements of shoaling fishes or flying S to feed in warmer waters off the W coast of Africa.

GREY HERON
Ardea cinerea

SIZE Length 90–98cm **HABITAT** Wide range of coastal and freshwater wetlands **FOOD** Fish, amphibians, invertebrates **VOICE** Harsh *crank* call, otherwise silent

IDENTIFICATION
Adult plumage is mostly grey on back and white on underside, with black areas on neck, head and 'shoulders'. A trailing crest of black feathers is usually present. Long legs and large feet are yellowish green, and dagger-shaped bill is large and yellow. Juveniles have more mottled grey plumage and a greyer bill.

LOCATION	DATE/TIME

STATUS AND HABITS

The typical pose of the Grey Heron is standing motionless in shallow water, bill poised ready to strike if prey comes close enough. Sometimes birds stalk slowly through the shallows, hoping to dislodge prey with their long toes. After feeding, Grey Herons normally preen themselves thoroughly, using the powdery feathers on the chest to help remove slime. Nests are built high in trees, often colonially, and breeding commences early in the year. A widespread bird, found in a wide range of coastal and fresh-water habitats, the Grey Heron will move to the coast in large numbers in freezing conditions.

KEY FACT

Grey Herons present a large outline when in flight, with huge, broad wings and slow, powerful wingbeats. The neck is kinked and the head drawn back to the body, but the legs trail behind.

LITTLE EGRET
Egretta garzetta

SIZE Length 55–65cm **HABITAT** Coastal lagoons, estuaries, marshes, lakes **FOOD** Fish, amphibians, aquatic invertebrates **VOICE** Mostly silent, but makes harsh *kraah* calls at breeding colonies

IDENTIFICATION

A pure white heron-like bird with a long, pointed black bill, black legs, and bright yellow feet with long toes. In breeding season, bare skin at base of bill becomes yellow, and long, elegant head plumes develop. In flight, head and neck are hunched up but legs trail behind and wings show a broad outline.

LOCATION	DATE/TIME

STATUS AND HABITS

The Little Egret is widespread across **S** Britain and Ireland, and occurs in any coastal and freshwater habitats that provide shallow water for wading and trees nearby for nesting. When hunched up in the resting position it is not an elegant bird, but when stalking prey it is very striking. It may wait, motionless for prey to swim by, or walk slowly, pushing its long toes through mud or weed to dislodge a fish, stabbing rapidly to capture it. Often solitary when feeding, Little Egrets usually nest in large colonies.

KEY FACT

Little Egrets were once hunted for their white head plumes, which were used by the millinery trade, but this practice was banned and the birds are now increasingly common throughout their range.

WHITE-TAILED EAGLE
Haliaeetus albicilla

SIZE **Wingspan 190–240cm** HABITAT **Sheltered rocky coasts and large lochs with trees or rocky cliffs for perching and nesting** FOOD **Fish, birds, mammals, carrion** VOICE **Loud, mournful yapping**

IDENTIFICATION

A huge, powerful raptor with long, parallel-sided wings. Adult plumage is essentially a slightly mottled brown with a paler head and neck, and a short white wedge-shaped tail. The huge hooked bill and powerful legs and feet are yellow. Juveniles have a dark tail and paler or white dappling on belly and underwings.

KEY FACT Breeding birds pair for life and construct huge twiggy nests in tall trees or on sea cliffs. Suitable nest sites are frequently reused each year, sometimes for many decades.

LOCATION	DATE/TIME

STATUS AND HABITS

Powerful and agile predators, White-tailed Eagles can snatch food from the surface of the water. Fish and seabirds feature heavily in their diet, but they readily take carrion when it is available. Intense persecution resulted in the extinction of the species in Britain in the early 19th century; small, stable breeding populations today are still centred around reintroduction sites on the NW coast of Scotland and the Hebrides. Territories are large and may include 70km of sheltered coast, but birds are sometimes also recorded over moorland habitats.

PEREGRINE
Falco peregrinus

FACT FILE

SIZE Wingspan 90–100cm **HABITAT** Nests on rocky sea cliffs, quarries, occasionally tall buildings **FOOD** Medium-sized birds **VOICE** Harsh, screaming *reeea-reee-reee* cry; loud *kek-kek-kek* alarm call

KEY FACT
Peregrines can reach speeds exceeding 240kph during their spectacular stoops. Nests on prominent landmarks (such as Chichester Cathedral) are closely monitored and observable by video-link **CCTV** cameras.

IDENTIFICATION
A large falcon with a relatively short, stocky body and broad, pointed wings. Adults have grey upperparts with pale barred underparts. Broad, dark moustachial stripes contrast with white cheeks and chin. Bright yellow eye-ring, cere and feet are sometimes obvious in good light. Juveniles are similar but have browner plumage overall and underparts suffused with buff-orange.

LOCATION	DATE/TIME

STATUS AND HABITS

Pesticide poisoning resulted in catastrophic population declines in the species in the 1960s, but bans on the use of organochlorine pesticides and protection from deliberate persecution have since led to dramatic recoveries. Peregrines favour undisturbed, inaccessible nest sites on cliffs and rocky outcrops, although man-made structures increasingly fulfil this requirement. Prey items include a variety of small to medium-sized birds, most caught on the wing over open habitats. Hunting Peregrines fly with stiff, rapid wingbeats and fold their wings back to perform 'power dives' onto unsuspecting prey.

JUVENILE

KESTREL
Falco tinnunculus

SIZE Wingspan 65–75cm **HABITAT** Open country, coastal cliffs, towns, roadsides **FOOD** Small mammals, some birds, amphibians, insects **VOICE** Shrill *kee-kee-kee* calls, often near nest site

IDENTIFICATION

A small bird of prey, often seen hovering, showing its long tail, downturned head and narrow wings. Male has a grey tail and head, brick-red spotted upperparts and a paler spotted underside. Female is more uniform in colour, with heavily spotted light chestnut plumage and a barred tail. At a distance, both sexes can appear similar. Juveniles resemble female.

KEY FACT Excellent eyesight enables Kestrels to hunt well into the dusk or in poor weather, in conditions when other birds of prey would have to give up.

MALE

LOCATION	DATE/TIME

STATUS AND HABITS

The Kestrel is one of the commonest birds of prey, seen in a wide range of open habitats including the coast, but especially grasslands where small mammals are common. Its ability to hover for prolonged spells enables it to hunt prey in the open; it drops rapidly when food is spotted and then flies off to a perch to eat it. Apart from hovering, Kestrels will also stalk food such as earthworms on the ground, or sit, in their characteristic upright posture, on posts or wires to look for prey.

FEMALE

OYSTERCATCHER
Haematopus ostralegus

SIZE Length 40–45cm **HABITAT** Rocky shores, estuaries, stony riverbeds and lake shores **FOOD** Molluscs, marine worms, earthworms **VOICE** Loud *kubeek kubeek* alarm notes; shrill piping calls

IDENTIFICATION

A large wading bird. Adults have striking black and white plumage, a red eye, a long orange-red bill and pinkish legs. Wings show a bold white wingbar in flight. In winter, a white chin stripe appears on black neck. Newly hatched chicks have excellent camouflage, resembling mossy rocks. Juvenile birds are paler than adults with more white on chin.

SUMMER

LOCATION	DATE/TIME

WINTER

KEY FACT

Males may gather in small groups in spring and perform a strange display, calling loudly and making a variety of clapping sounds with their heads pointing downwards.

STATUS AND HABITS

Familiar as coastal birds, often roosting in large flocks at high tide, Oystercatchers are also found far inland nesting along stony riverbeds, islands in gravel pits or around large lakes, and feeding in damp ground in open fields, golf courses and marshes. Their loud calls can be heard night and day as they aggressively chase predators. The long bill enables them to probe damp ground for earthworms and invertebrates. Inland birds will migrate a short distance to nearby coastal areas in the winter.

AVOCET
Recurvirostra avosetta

FACT FILE

SIZE **Length 42–46cm** HABITAT **Coastal lagoons, estuaries, marshes** FOOD **Small aquatic invertebrates** VOICE **Various shrill calls, including a piping *pleet pleet***

IDENTIFICATION

A very distinctive large black and white wader with a slender, upcurved bill and long blue-grey legs. Adult plumage is mostly pure white with a black head and nape, and black patches on wing that have an oval shape in flight. From below, Avocets look mostly white, apart from black wingtips. Juveniles resemble adults but have a brownish head and nape.

KEY FACT Avocets are excellent parents, tending their young carefully and guiding them to the best feeding areas. They will aggressively chase off predators such as gulls and corvids.

LOCATION	DATE/TIME

STATUS AND HABITS

The characteristic feeding behaviour of the **Avocet** is to sweep its bill from side to side through liquid mud to catch tiny invertebrates. The long legs enable it to wade easily, but it can also upend itself like a duck in deeper water to reach the best feeding areas. Nests are built colonially on shingle banks close to good feeding areas, and are usually lined with shells or small stones. After the breeding season, most Avocets migrate to sheltered estuaries and bays where mud remains ice-free.

LAPWING
Vanellus vanellus

FACT FILE

SIZE **Length 28–31cm** HABITAT **Coastal marshes, wet grasslands, farmland pastures** FOOD **Soil invertebrates, especially earthworms, beetles, larvae** VOICE **Shrill *peeoo-wit* calls; various contact notes**

IDENTIFICATION

Once known as the Green Plover, the Lapwing has glossy green upperparts, an all-white underside and orange undertail coverts, shown clearly when head is lowered for feeding and tail is raised. Both sexes have long crest and are similar, but in spring male has a black chin and throat. In flight, broad wings have a rounded profile and show bold black and white patterning. Winter adults have pale margins to feathers, giving a scalloped effect to back and wings. Juveniles are similar but with a browner chest and shorter crest.

LOCATION	DATE/TIME

STATUS AND HABITS

Lapwings perform acrobatic aerial displays over their breeding sites in spring, with energetic diving and swooping, accompanied by the far-carrying *pee-wit* calls. This manoeuvrability can also help outwit predators, and Lapwings vigorously defend their young against intruders. Open fields and grassland are favoured nesting sites, sometimes well away from water. In winter Lapwings gather in larger flocks, closer to the coast.

KEY FACT

Damper areas provide the best feeding for Lapwings, and birds will often feed at night when invertebrates are more active.

GOLDEN PLOVER
Pluvialis apricaria

FACT FILE

SIZE Length 26–29cm **HABITAT** Breeds on upland bogs and moorland; winters on coastal and lowland pastures
FOOD Soil invertebrates, some fruits and seeds
VOICE Plaintive, whistling *pyuuh-pu* calls

IDENTIFICATION

A medium-sized, plump wader with a rounded head, short bill and dark legs. Adult winter plumage is spangled golden brown above and pale below. Breeding male has a black face and black underside edged with white. Breeding female is similar but with less black and a greyer face. Juveniles resemble winter adults but may show faint barring below.

SUMMER FEMALE

LOCATION	DATE/TIME

STATUS AND HABITS

Golden Plovers prefer to feed on short, damp grassland, where they can run around in pursuit of insects and earthworms. Excellent camouflage enables them to feed and nest safely on the ground, and they take flight only if approached closely. Scattered pairs nest on open moorland and upland grassland, but birds gather in larger flocks in autumn, moving to favoured overwintering areas (sometimes with Lapwings) on grass airfields and coastal grazing marshes.

JUVENILE

KEY FACT

The plain white underwing shows clearly in flight and is a good identification feature for separating Golden Plover from the very similar Grey Plover, which has a black underwing.

GREY PLOVER
Pluvialis squatarola

SIZE Length 27–29cm HABITAT Large sandy and muddy estuaries, harbours FOOD Shellfish, marine worms, other invertebrates VOICE Distinctive *pee-oo-ee* whistle, repeated three times

IDENTIFICATION

A medium-sized, plump wader with a short, stocky bill and a uniform grey appearance when seen at a distance. Adult winter plumage is variable, generally comprising pale grey underparts with pale-spangled, dark grey-black upperparts. Summer adults develop black underparts, most striking in males. Juveniles are more buff coloured. In flight, presence of black armpits (axillaries) distinguishes the species from the similar-looking Golden Plover.

KEY FACT
Young birds do not breed until they are two years old. Many non-breeding birds will often remain on the wintering grounds throughout the year.

WINTER

LOCATION	DATE/TIME

STATUS AND HABITS

Exclusively coastal, the Grey Plover is a non-breeding winter visitor to the region, with over 50,000 birds overwintering on estuaries and mudflats around Britain's coasts. Adult birds return from their breeding grounds in the high Arctic as early as Jul, with juveniles arriving from Aug–Sep onwards. Grey Plovers are typically less gregarious than other waders but frequently mix with large flocks of small waders at high-tide roosts. They forage on beaches and open flats at low tide in search of molluscs and marine worms.

WINTER

WINTER

RINGED PLOVER
Charadrius hiaticula

FACT FILE

SIZE Length 16–19cm **HABITAT** Sandy or gravelly shores, estuaries, mudflats; increasingly on flooded gravel pits **FOOD** Variety of small invertebrates **VOICE** Gentle *tuu-eep*, repeated rapidly when alarmed

IDENTIFICATION

A small wader with orange legs and a short orange bill with a black tip. Breeding adults have sandy-brown upperparts and white underparts, with a continuous dark collar and striking black and white facial markings (more subdued in females). In winter, black markings fade to dull brown. In flight, distinctive broad white bands are visible on wings. Juveniles resemble winter adults, but duller brown on head and breast, bill all dark and legs more yellowish.

KEY FACT Ringed Plover eggs are extremely well camouflaged and very difficult to spot if the adult leaves the nest unattended. Adult birds will often feign a broken wing to lure potential predators away from the nest.

LOCATION	DATE/TIME

STATUS AND HABITS

A resident breeding bird, present year-round in suitable habitats throughout the region. It nests on the ground, favouring sandy or shingle beaches, but human disturbance is usually a limiting factor in determining the suitability of many potential nesting areas. Birds increasingly nest on inland gravel pits where human access is limited. Winter populations are boosted by an influx of passage birds from Europe, Greenland and Canada. Ringed Plovers feed on open beaches and mudflats, running in short bursts, typically punctuated with brief pauses, before snatching at invertebrates on or near the ground.

LITTLE RINGED PLOVER
Charadrius dubius

FACT FILE

SIZE Length 14–15cm **HABITAT** Large stony riverbeds, lake shores, gravel pits **FOOD** Aquatic invertebrates, insects, spiders **VOICE** Mournful-sounding *kree-u kree-u* and shrill *kiu* flight calls

IDENTIFICATION
A small, well-camouflaged wader. Adults have dull sandy-brown upperparts, a pure white underside, and a boldly patterned black and white head. Black eye is surrounded by a bright yellow eye-ring. Bill is black and legs are a dull flesh colour. In flight, wings look plain, lacking any wingbar. Juveniles look like faded versions of adults.

LOCATION	DATE/TIME

KEY FACT If disturbed by a predator, a nesting bird will perform an elaborate and convincing wing-dragging or feeding display in order to distract attention away from its eggs or chicks.

STATUS AND HABITS

Little Ringed Plovers arrive in early spring from overwintering sites in Africa. Initially lingering on shingle beaches near the coast, they move inland to gravel pits, riverbeds and lakes, where they become very secretive as they start breeding, revealing their presence only with their plaintive calls. They have adapted well to activities such as gravel extraction and reservoir construction, readily taking to man-made sites. They avoid dense vegetation and very wet marshland, preferring stony open sites in the **S**.

LITTLE STINT
Calidris minuta

FACT FILE

SIZE Length 12–14cm **HABITAT** Winter visitor on marshes and lake shores **FOOD** Aquatic invertebrates in winter **VOICE** Thin, piping *svee svee svee* display calls; quiet *tip* contact notes

IDENTIFICATION

A very small wader with a short black bill and legs. Adult winter plumage is mostly grey-buff above and white below, but in summer upperparts are rusty red, crown is darker and cheeks are reddish. Upper feathers have dark centres and pale margins. Juveniles resemble adults but show a white 'V' pattern on upperparts.

KEY FACT This is the smallest European sandpiper, so can be distinguished by size, but beware confusion with the only slightly larger Temminck's Stint, which also stops off here on migration.

SUMMER

LOCATION	DATE/TIME

STATUS AND HABITS

This diminutive wader often feeds among other small species like the Dunlin, but is less likely to enter the water and is usually a more active feeder, scurrying around in search of moving prey, which it captures with quick stabs of the bill. It prefers to feed in sheltered backwaters and creeks, avoiding more open sites. As a passage migrant from its breeding grounds on the Arctic tundra, it is most likely to be seen in spring and autumn, and only in ones and twos, never in large flocks.

JUVENILE

DUNLIN
Calidris alpina

FACT FILE

SIZE Length 16–22cm **HABITAT** Breeds on moorlands and Arctic tundra; overwinters on sandy shores and lakes **FOOD** Insects in summer; small invertebrates in winter **VOICE** Trilling display over nest sites; harsh *krreee* in flight

IDENTIFICATION

A small wader. Winter adults have mostly grey-brown plumage above and a pale underside. Summer adults have slightly browner upperparts and belly is black. In flight, a distinct white wingbar can be seen. All Dunlin have a slightly downcurved black bill, but its length varies according to race. Juveniles resemble moulting adults, but breast is streaked and upperparts are paler owing to buff feather margins.

SUMMER

LOCATION	DATE/TIME

STATUS AND HABITS

The Dunlin is one of the commonest waders to be seen in winter in Britain, but many are also present in summer, nesting on moors and uplands in the region. In winter they migrate to coasts and marshes, joined by birds from further N. In the breeding season they tend to be solitary and secretive, revealing their presence only by the male's trilling display calls. In winter they congregate in large flocks, often flying in formation, wheeling and turning together, the flocks changing colour from grey to white.

WINTER

KEY FACT Dunlin that breed in Britain and Ireland have a slightly shorter bill and smaller black belly patch than birds from elsewhere in Europe, and can usually be picked out in mixed flocks.

CURLEW SANDPIPER
Calidris ferruginea

FACT FILE

SIZE Length 18–20cm HABITAT Passage migrant seen on coasts and large lakes FOOD Tiny molluscs in winter VOICE *Krillee* flight calls, otherwise silent

IDENTIFICATION

In summer plumage adults are striking, with a rich red underside and darker mottled upperparts. Newly moulted plumage has mealy appearance owing to unworn pale feather margins. Bill is black and downcurved, legs are relatively long and black, and white rump patch and pale wingbar show in flight. Juveniles have much paler buff-orange upperparts and chest, pale underside and pale eye-stripe.

KEY FACT Curlew Sandpipers have the ability to deposit body fat very quickly, so a few days' non-stop feeding on tiny invertebrates will provide enough reserves for the next stage of a long migration.

SUMMER

LOCATION	DATE/TIME

STATUS AND HABITS

Curlew Sandpipers make long migrations from their overwintering sites
in tropical Africa to their high Arctic breeding grounds, and a few birds
may stop off in spring on coasts and marshes in the E Mediterranean
or even in Britain. They are more likely to be seen here on their return
migration in autumn, when some take a more **W** route. At this time they
may join with Dunlin on coasts and marshes, when they can be picked out
by their larger size and longer, more curved bill; many of these birds will
be juveniles with paler plumage.

JUVENILE

PURPLE SANDPIPER
Calidris maritima

SIZE Length 21cm **HABITAT** Breeds on moors and tundra; winters on rocky shores and stony beaches
FOOD Invertebrates, some plant material
VOICE Sharp *kwit* in flight; low *we-weet* call

FACT FILE

IDENTIFICATION

A medium-sized wader with a downcurved beak and short yellowish-orange legs, appearing larger, darker and more portly than a Dunlin.

WINTER

Winter adults have a grey head, breast and upperparts, and are generally dark grey on back with pale underparts and grey streaking in flanks. Summer adults show reddish-brown markings on the back and a paler face. Juveniles resemble winter adults, but with a more scaly appearance and more rufous on crown and mantle.

KEY FACT Purple Sandpipers are well camouflaged against the mottled grey backdrop of our rocky coasts and are easily overlooked. Feeding birds are often very confiding and can be watched at close range for prolonged periods.

LOCATION	DATE/TIME

STATUS AND HABITS

Although a handful of pairs (fewer than five) nest each year on remote Scottish moors, most of the birds seen in the region are wintering birds from N Europe and the Arctic. More than 15,000 winter on British coasts each year, feeding alone or in small, unobtrusive flocks along the 'splash zone' of exposed rocky headlands. They happily brave the most thunderous waves and surf to snatch invertebrates and molluscs dislodged from rock crevices and gullies.

WINTER

SANDERLING
Calidris alba

SIZE Length 18–20cm HABITAT Winter visitor on sandy beaches and mudflats FOOD Small invertebrates, some plant material VOICE Excited *plit* call

IDENTIFICATION

A small, energetic wader with black legs and bill. Winter adults appear very pale, generally grey above with bright white underparts. Summer adults (occasionally seen here in late spring and early autumn) show a chestnut flush on head and neck, and dark-centred feathers across back. Juveniles resemble winter adults, but scapulars and mantle are spotted with black and white.

WINTER

LOCATION	DATE/TIME

STATUS AND HABITS

Breeding on coastal tundra in the high Arctic, the Sanderling is a non-breeding winter visitor and passage migrant in spring and autumn in our region. Approximately 20,000 birds winter in Britain, but they are frequently seen throughout the year, often in small flocks, favouring long, sandy beaches and estuary mudflats. They feed very close to the water's edge, snatching small marine worms, crustaceans and molluscs that are disturbed by moving tides, looking like clockwork toys as they tirelessly run in and out along the foamy margin of breaking waves.

KEY FACT

This is one of the easiest small waders to identify, with its distinctive behaviour and very pale appearance. Note also the striking white wingbar in flight.

WINTER

KNOT
Calidris canutus

FACT FILE

SIZE Length 23–25cm HABITAT Winter visitor on large estuaries and mudflats FOOD Shellfish, marine worms, some plant material VOICE Repeated *kwet* call

IDENTIFICATION

A medium-sized, dumpy wader with relatively short legs and a stout bill. Its plumage is variable and generally lacks distinctive features. Winter adults appear rather grey, with uniformly grey upperparts and white underparts. Summer adults have a brick-red face, chest and belly, and feathers on back have black and chestnut centres and grey margins. Juveniles appear scaly.

KEY FACT Knots frequently forage close to the tide-line; the species' scientific name of *canutus* is a reference to King Canute, who famously tried to hold back the tide.

JUVENILE

LOCATION	DATE/TIME

STATUS AND HABITS

A non-breeding winter visitor and passage migrant to Britain from its Arctic tundra breeding grounds. Large estuaries and mudflats around the coasts of Britain and Ireland are vitally important feeding areas for migrating and wintering birds, the latter numbering over 250,000. Individual flocks may contain many tens of thousands of individuals, which fly in spectacular smoke-like formations around high-tide roost sites. The Wash is a good place to observe high concentrations of Knots, particularly during periods of cold weather.

SUMMER

GREENSHANK
Tringa nebularia

SIZE **Length 30–35cm** HABITAT **Breeds on bogs and marshes; overwinters on coastal estuaries, brackish pools and marshes** FOOD **Aquatic and terrestrial invertebrates, tiny fish, tadpoles** VOICE **Clear three-note *chew-chew-chew* calls**

IDENTIFICATION

Looking grey and white from a distance, adult Greenshanks in breeding plumage have darker markings on upperparts and arrow-shaped markings on chest, giving them a streaked appearance. In winter, underside is pure white, and upperparts have a slightly scaly appearance due to paler feather margins. Juveniles resemble winter adults, but with browner plumage and more defined streaks on neck and breast.

KEY FACT In flight, the Greenshank's wings look all dark with no wingbars, but there is a narrow, pale rump patch that extends along the back.

WINTER

LOCATION	DATE/TIME

STATUS AND HABITS

The Greenshank is a scarce breeding bird in **N** Scotland, but a frequent
passage migrant in autumn and a regular winter visitor to coasts and
marshes. Usually fairly solitary, it prefers sheltered creeks and backwaters,
and small marshy pools where it can hunt prey such as small fish. Running
through the shallows with the slightly upcurved bill held underwater is a
favourite method of catching small fish like sticklebacks, which are lifted
out of the water before being swallowed.

JUVENILE

REDSHANK
Tringa totanus

FACT FILE

SIZE Length 24–27cm HABITAT Sheltered estuaries and mudflats, marshes, wet meadows FOOD Marine invertebrates, insect larvae, earthworms VOICE Two-note *tu-hu* call; *tyoo tyoo tyoo* flight call; louder *klu-klu-klu* alarm call

IDENTIFICATION

Adults in all plumages have long orange-red legs and a reddish base to long bill. Winter adults are mostly grey-brown above and pale below. Breeding adults have darker upperparts with browner patches in feathers, N birds being darker than those from the S. Juveniles are similar to winter adults but legs are dull orange and underside has a slightly barred appearance.

WINTER

LOCATION	DATE/TIME

STATUS AND HABITS

In the breeding season, the male Redshank will display by rising and falling on rapid wingbeats, giving the far-carrying *tyoo tyoo tyoo* call. When landing, he stands briefly with wings raised, showing the pure white underside. Birds also give a shrill alarm call at any sign of danger, meriting their old name of Warden of the Marshes. Nests are built in clumps of grass, and newly hatched young are tended by both parents. After the breeding season most birds migrate to the coast.

KEY FACT In flight in all plumages, the wings look darker at the tip and outer edges and show a white trailing edge, and juveniles resemble adults.

WINTER

SPOTTED REDSHANK
Tringa erythropus

FACT FILE

SIZE Length 29–32cm HABITAT Passage migrant and scarce winter visitor to estuaries and marshes FOOD Small terrestrial and aquatic invertebrates VOICE Repetitive, whirring *kruu-ee* display calls; shrill *chu-witt* flight calls

IDENTIFICATION

An elegant wader with long red legs and a long bill. Breeding adults are mostly sooty black with pale margins to feathers on upperparts (these rise to its common name), and bill and legs are brighter red in summer. Winter birds are pale grey-brown above and white below. Juveniles resemble winter adults but with grey barring below.

KEY FACT

In flight, Spotted Redshanks show a narrow, wedge-shaped white rump patch, but no wingbar, easily distinguishing them from the similar Redshank. The shrill call also differs from that of the Redshank.

WINTER

LOCATION	DATE/TIME

STATUS AND HABITS

Spotted Redshanks nest on bogs and tundra in the Arctic, with the males helping with every stage of rearing young, including incubation. Females leave breeding areas long before males. A few overwinter here on marshes and estuaries where they can find soft mud to feed in, often returning year after year to the same place. Feeding in shallow water, often in small groups, they make distinctive downwards stabbing movements with the long bill, sometimes venturing into quite deep water and upending like ducks.

WINTER

COMMON SANDPIPER
Actitis hypoleucos

FACT FILE

SIZE Length 19–21cm **HABITAT** Stony shorelines; sheltered coasts in winter **FOOD** Aquatic insects and other invertebrates **VOICE** Shrill, rapid *hee dee dee* flight and alarm calls; rhythmic *will-he-wicket* display song

IDENTIFICATION
Adults look plain grey-buff above at a distance, but in fact have delicately patterned upperparts with fine markings that fade in winter. Underside is pure white with a distinct white shoulder patch. Legs are grey-green, and short bill is dark brown with a hint of yellow at base. Juveniles have a scaly appearance, resulting from pale feather margins.

KEY FACT When disturbed, the Common Sandpiper will fly off low over the water, almost touching it with its wings, and gives its shrill alarm call. The dark wings show a narrow white bar.

JUVENILE

LOCATION	DATE/TIME

STATUS AND HABITS

The Common Sandpiper is a widespread resident wader, found in a great range of freshwater habitats across Britain and Europe. It usually feeds actively at the edge of a lake or river, constantly bobbing up and down and making short dashes after prey, which it stabs swiftly with its bill. Nests are built on the ground near water and newly hatched young are taken to water to be fed. In winter, there is a general migration S, but some birds remain near the breeding sites.

WINTER

TURNSTONE
Arenaria interpres

FACT FILE

SIZE Length 23cm HABITAT Non-breeding visitor to beaches, estuaries, rocky shores FOOD Predominantly invertebrates; will sometimes scavenge scraps and even carrion VOICE Twittering *trk-ititit*; staccato *tuc-tuc-tuc* in flight

IDENTIFICATION

A robust wader with bright orange legs and a stout triangular bill. Its contrasting black and white plumage pattern is distinctive in flight. Summer adults are most striking, with bold black and white head markings, a black breast-band, white underparts and a mottled chestnut-brown and black back. Winter birds become more brown, including face and neck, but retain dark breast and white underparts. Juveniles resemble winter adults but upperparts appear scalier.

WINTER

LOCATION	DATE/TIME

STATUS AND HABITS

Commonly encountered on a variety of coastal habitats throughout Britain and often present year-round, the Turnstone is essentially a non-breeding visitor to our region, although it is suspected that a few birds occasionally nest in Scotland. Small flocks often associate with similar-sized waders such as Ringed Plovers and Purple Sandpipers. Birds systematically creep over seaweed-covered rocks or along strand-lines, turning over weed and rocks in search of small invertebrates. Feeding birds are often indifferent around humans, sometimes scavenging food scraps around busy beachside cafés.

KEY FACT

Turnstones are aptly named, being capable of turning over stones equal to their own bodyweight. Up to 50,000 birds may be present along our coastline between Sep and Apr.

WINTER

WHIMBREL
Numenius phaeopus

SIZE Length 40–45cm **HABITAT** Breeds on
moorland; passage migrant on mudflats and coastal marshes
FOOD Mainly invertebrates, some plant material **VOICE** Plaintive
bubbling, comprising seven drawn-out, slightly ascending notes

FACT FILE

IDENTIFICATION

A smaller, less robust cousin of the similar-looking Curlew, and with an
appreciably smaller, downcurved bill. All birds are predominately grey-buff
with dark brown streaks; they are distinguished from similar species by a
dark eye-stripe, pale supercilium and dark brown crown with a pale median
stripe, giving head a distinctly stripy appearance. Pale rump and back are
clearly visible in flight.

LOCATION	DATE/TIME

Whimbrels are most often seen feeding solitarily or in small, loosely associated groups, although migrating birds sometimes travel in larger flocks of 100-plus birds. Distant birds are usually heard before they are seen.

STATUS AND HABITS

This migratory species breeds in the Arctic and winters on the coasts of Africa, although several hundred pairs also nest in Scotland; the boggy moorlands of Shetland and Orkney provide the best place to spot birds during the breeding season. The species is, however, more frequently seen as a passage migrant around our coasts, particularly in Apr and Sep, when they stop to feed on open marshes and mudflats. Most food items are snatched from near the surface; birds rarely use their long bill to probe deep into the mud.

CURLEW
Numenius arquata

FACT FILE

SIZE Length 50–60cm **HABITAT** Upland moors and bogs in breeding season; coastal flats and marshes in winter
FOOD Earthworms, soil invertebrates, molluscs, crustaceans on coasts
VOICE Mournful *cour-lee* calls; melodious, bubbling trill when breeding

IDENTIFICATION

A large wader with a long, downcurved bill, longer in female, which is also a larger bird; otherwise, sexes are similar. Adults have mottled brown plumage and paler undersides. Summer plumage has a more yellow tone than in winter and bill is all dark. In winter, lower mandible is pinkish brown. Juveniles resemble winter adults.

STATUS AND HABITS

The unmistakable ringing call of the Curlew is as evocative of wild bogs and marshes in spring as it is of estuaries and wetlands in winter. In the breeding season birds will be fairly solitary and secretive, nesting in tussocks on bogs and guarding their chicks until they can fly. In autumn they will gather in large flocks and move to marshes and coasts, where they feed in muddy areas on a wide range of invertebrates. They are vocal through the year, calling in flight and on the ground.

LOCATION	DATE/TIME

KEY FACT

The long, curved bill of the **Curlew** is the perfect implement for probing soft mud and extracting burrowing prey. They are also adept at removing the soft bodies of molluscs from their shells.

WINTER

BLACK-TAILED GODWIT
Limosa limosa

FACT FILE

SIZE Length 36–44cm HABITAT Breeds on damp meadows and marshes; overwinters on sheltered coasts and coastal lagoons FOOD Invertebrates VOICE Usually quiet, but on nest site gives rapid, nasal *kee wee wee wee* calls

IDENTIFICATION

A large wader with long legs and a long, straight bill. Breeding adults have a brick-red head and neck, and chest and upperparts are mottled with black, chestnut and grey, giving appearance of broken dark bars, especially on upper chest. Underside is mostly pale grey. Winter birds are pale grey above and white below. In flight, upperwings show a white wingbar. Juveniles resemble winter adults but have more brown-buff tones.

KEY FACT The amount of red on the head and neck is variable, with some birds very pale in summer, but all birds show a half black and half white tail, and bold white wingbars.

MOULTING

LOCATION	DATE/TIME

STATUS AND HABITS

Freshwater marshes, especially if grazed by cattle and intersected by ditches, are favoured breeding sites for Black-tailed Godwits, and they often nest semi-colonially. Once large enough, young birds are taken to muddy shores or estuaries, where the feeding is more productive. Long legs enable the birds to wade in quite deep water, and the long bill can probe the mud to depths other waders cannot reach. The tip of the bill is sensitive and also slightly flexible, allowing the bird to detect prey and extract it from the mud.

WINTER

BAR-TAILED GODWIT
Limosa lapponica

FACT FILE

SIZE Length 35–40cm HABITAT Winter visitor to
estuaries and sheltered muddy/sandy shores FOOD Molluscs,
worms, crustaceans VOICE Nasal *kve-wee* in flight

IDENTIFICATION
Similar to Black-tailed Godwit, but with shorter legs, an upcurved bill
and a barred tail; also lacks a white wingbar in flight. Winter adults are
grey-brown, appearing mottled on back, faintly streaked on flanks, breast
and neck, and with an off-white belly. Summer male develops unbarred,
wholly orange-brown underparts. Summer female is flushed with apricot
on head, breast and flanks. Juveniles resemble winter adults but have
more buff on head and neck.

WINTER

LOCATION	DATE/TIME

STATUS AND HABITS

A non-breeding winter visitor to the region's coasts, with tens of thousands of birds present between Sep and Apr. They typically favour large, open tidal estuaries and flats with sandy or muddy substrates, where they feed by probing their long bills deep into the wet sediments in search of molluscs and large marine worms. Our visitors' breeding range extends from N Scandinavia to Siberia, with pairs usually nesting on boggy moorland and tundra.

WINTER

KEY FACT

Females are generally larger than males and are often the most difficult individuals to separate from similar-sized Black-tailed Godwits. Migrating Bar-tailed Godwits can fly non-stop for eight days and cover an astonishing 11,000km.

RUFF
Philomachus pugnax

FACT FILE

SIZE Length 26–32cm **HABITAT** Muddy shorelines, sheltered coastal lagoons, wet meadows, marshes, swamps
FOOD Variety of invertebrates from soil and water margins
VOICE Usually silent, but may make quiet squeaks

IDENTIFICATION

An unusual wader with great variations in plumage; male is much larger than female. Winter adults are mostly mottled brownish buff above, buff on chest and pale below. Dark bill is slightly downcurved and legs are reddish. Breeding male has elaborate head and neck feathers that fluff out to form a ruff; this varies between individuals. Breeding female has mostly buff upperparts with variable mottling and streaking, and a paler underside. Juveniles resemble winter adults but with more buff colours.

FEMALE

SPOTTER'S CHART

LOCATION	DATE/TIME

STATUS AND HABITS

In spring, male **Ruffs** gather in leks near their nesting sites and strut around displaying their colourful breeding plumage, each male trying to outdo the others with its appearance and its elaborate dance, leaping into the air, or sometimes freezing in one position to show its colours to best effect. The much plainer and smaller females watch closely. Nesting semi-colonially, pairs choose large freshwater marshes as breeding sites. By late summer the males will have moulted into their more uniform plumage.

MALE

KEY FACT

In autumn, flocks made up mostly of juveniles gather on coastal marshes before heading to Africa for the winter. On their return migration in spring, some males may already be showing their breeding colours.

GREY PHALAROPE
Phalaropus fulicarius

FACT FILE

SIZE Length 20–22cm **HABITAT** Mainly pelagic
passage migrant; occasionally turns up on inland lakes
FOOD Small invertebrates, marine plankton
VOICE Sharp *pit* in flight; generally silent in region

IDENTIFICATION

A small wader, typically seen in Britain in its winter plumage (same in
both sexes): essentially grey above and white below, with a dark smudge
through eye. Bill is shorter and stouter than that of other phalaropes, and
yellow with a black tip. Breeding female has red underparts with a dark
crown and white face patch. Breeding male is similar but duller and more
dappled. Juveniles resemble winter adults, with a light buff wash on neck
and breast, and a scaly-looking mantle and scapulars.

KEY FACT   In North America this species is known as the
Red Phalarope, a reference to its bold breeding plumage. Flocks of
Grey Phalaropes will often feed on krill driven to the surface by
lunge-feeding whales.

WINTER

LOCATION	DATE/TIME

STATUS AND HABITS

A passage migrant off coasts in our region, the Grey Phalarope is most frequently seen in autumn and spring, occasionally turning up on inland lakes after winter storms. It nests on Arctic shores, where the males incubate and care for the young. Adults spend much of their lives at sea, often converging at ocean upwellings where zooplankton are brought close to the surface. Feeding birds generally swim on the surface, usually in tight, rapid circles, snatching at prey items stirred up by their tiny feet.

FIRST WINTER

SNIPE
Gallinago gallinago

FACT FILE

SIZE **Length 25–27cm** HABITAT **Coastal marshes, bogs, damp meadows** FOOD **Soil and freshwater invertebrates** VOICE *Tic-a-tic* calls in breeding season; sneeze-like alarm call

IDENTIFICATION

A dumpy wader with a very long bill, brown at tip and paler at base, and dull green legs. Upperparts are brown with pale stripes, these more clearly defined on head; larger feathers have dark centres and pale margins, giving a scaly appearance and providing excellent camouflage. Flanks are barred and underside is greyish white. Short tail is barred, with a buff margin.

LOCATION	DATE/TIME

STATUS AND HABITS

The long bill is used to probe soft mud in a distinctive jerky action, the tip vibrating slightly to disturb and detect food, which can be sucked up without removing the bill from the mud. If alarmed, Snipe will fly off rapidly on a jerky flight path and drop quickly out of sight. They can also remain motionless for long periods, relying on camouflage for protection. In spring they are obvious by their displays, but at other times Snipe are very secretive, often seen only when flushed suddenly.

KEY FACT

In spring, males perform an exciting display flight, climbing high and then swooping down with splayed tail feathers, which create a curious bleating or drumming sound.

GREAT SKUA
Stercorarius skua

FACT FILE

SIZE Length 50–60cm HABITAT Breeds on coastal moorland; pelagic for much of year FOOD Fish, birds, carrion VOICE Mainly silent

IDENTIFICATION

A bulky brown seabird with distinctive flashes of white on wing. Adults sport a rich chocolate-brown plumage mottled with pale buff streaks and a distinctly golden mane. Legs and powerful-looking bill are black. Juveniles generally lack the pale mottling of adults.

ADULTS DISPLAYING

STATUS AND HABITS

Great Skuas are competent predators but readily scavenge carrion from the surface of the sea. They are notorious pirates, revelling in snatching fish from large seabirds, sometimes bullying them continuously until they regurgitate their last meal. Nearly 10,000 birds breed in loose colonies on the coastal moorlands of islands in the far N of Britain. From spring to autumn birds can be seen along our coasts, usually as they migrate S to their wintering grounds on the coasts of S Europe and Africa.

LOCATION	DATE/TIME

KEY FACT

Great Skuas
are affectionately known
to birdwatchers by their
Shetland name of Bonxie.
They are dedicated parents,
fearlessly protective of their
nests, and will ferociously
dive-bomb and attack humans
if they venture too close.

ARCTIC SKUA
Stercorarius parasiticus

SIZE Length 42–58cm **HABITAT** Breeds on coastal
moors and tundra; coastal or pelagic on migration **FOOD** Fish, small
birds, mammals, insects **VOICE** Mostly silent; nasal wailing uttered
in display

FACT FILE

IDENTIFICATION

An elegant falcon-like seabird with pointed wings and extended tail feathers
that form a sharp 'double-point' at centre of tail. Adults occur in two
distinct colour morphs. Dark-phase adults appear uniformly grey-brown.
Pale-phase adults sport a similar-coloured plumage apart from a contrasting
white belly, breast and neck. Juveniles resemble dark-phase adults.

KEY FACT

Orkney and Shetland are strongholds for most of the
region's Arctic Skuas, but autumn seawatches from exposed coastal
headlands further S can also prove successful, particularly when a
strong onshore wind is blowing.

PALE PHASE

LOCATION	DATE/TIME

STATUS AND HABITS

A few thousand pairs breed on coastal moors and islands in the far N of Scotland. On passage, birds can be seen further S from coastal headlands as they head to wintering grounds on the coast of Africa and S Europe. Arctic Skuas use their extraordinary speed and agility to torment and terrorise smaller seabirds, particularly terns, to rob them of their catches. They rarely fish for themselves, and their pelagic winter distribution generally reflects the movements of the birds they scavenge from.

DARK PHASE

KITTIWAKE
Rissa tridactyla

SIZE Length 38–42cm **HABITAT** Mainly pelagic;
nests on coastal cliff ledges, sometimes man-made structures
FOOD Small fish, marine invertebrates **VOICE** Endearing kazoo-like
voice; often repeated *kitti-waake-kitte-waake* call near nest sites

IDENTIFICATION

A medium-sized, neat-looking gull with a small yellow bill, short black
legs and very distinctive black wingtips (like they have been dipped in ink).
Adults have blue-grey on back, a white head and white underparts; in winter
they may develop dark smudges behind eye. Juveniles have distinctive
V-shaped black stripes on top of each wing.

LOCATION	DATE/TIME

KEY FACT

Over 300,000 pairs nest in Britain, but the success of individual colonies often depends on the health of inshore fish stocks (particularly the abundance of sandeels). In some areas, Kittiwake colonies are now in decline.

STATUS AND HABITS

A pelagic species, common offshore along the coasts of the region, and coming closer to shore only to breed. Kittiwakes nest in large, noisy colonies, typically on coastal cliff ledges, and colonies are frequently associated with other cliff-nesting seabirds. They will occasionally nest on the walls of dockside warehouses or derelict harbour buildings, but are strictly coastal. Birds in established colonies can become accustomed to human observers and at some sites it is possible to watch birds at close range without causing disturbance.

COMMON GULL
Larus canus

FACT FILE

SIZE Length 38–44cm **HABITAT** Coasts, marshes, lakes, large rivers **FOOD** Marine invertebrates, fish, insects, earthworms **VOICE** Harsh *keeoow* and mewing *gleeoo* calls

IDENTIFICATION

A medium-sized gull, pale grey above and pure white below, with yellowish-green legs and a yellow bill. Adults have black wingtips with white patches, and grey-brown flecks on head and neck in winter. Immatures show more brown in wings in their first winter and a black tail band. Bill is black at first, becomes dull flesh colour and then yellow in second winter.

KEY FACT The Common Gull is smaller and more compact than the Herring Gull, has a dark eye with a red eye-ring, and lacks the orange spot on the bill.

WINTER

LOCATION	DATE/TIME

STATUS AND HABITS

Despite its name, this is not the commonest gull in Britain, nesting mainly in the **N** and dispersing in winter, when it is more widespread. Although it can feed at sea among other gulls, it is equally at home on land or freshwater sites, and is skilled at capturing cranefly larvae and earthworms, often by following the plough on farmland. The Common Gull population increased in the 20th century because the species has been able to adapt to changing land use.

WINTER

BLACK-HEADED GULL
Larus ridibundus

SIZE Length 38–44cm HABITAT Sheltered coasts, marshes, lakes, urban sites, farmland FOOD Insects, earthworms, marine and freshwater invertebrates, food scraps VOICE Harsh screeching calls, especially in nesting colonies

IDENTIFICATION

Summer adults have a chocolate-brown head, white nape, red bill with a black tip and red legs. Wings show a white leading edge in flight and black tips to primaries. In winter, adults' head is white, with two dark smudges behind eye; legs and bill are paler red than in summer. Juveniles have browner areas in wings and a black terminal tail band. Bill and legs are a dark flesh colour in first-winter birds, becoming redder in second year.

SUMMER

LOCATION	DATE/TIME

KEY FACT

In winter, Black-headed Gulls may congregate in huge roosts at dusk, converging from a wide area and often mixing with larger gulls; their distinctive head patterning at this time of year is a useful aid to identification.

STATUS AND HABITS

WINTER

A common and widespread species, sometimes found in large colonies on inland marshes as well as on coasts. As opportunist feeders, Black-headed Gulls are able to exploit many food sources provided in urban areas and the countryside, and can be seen on rubbish tips, reservoirs, farmland and city centres. Plentiful food supplies through the year have enabled the population to increase and spread its range.

MEDITERRANEAN GULL
Larus melanocephalus

FACT FILE

SIZE Length 37cm HABITAT Sheltered coasts, estuaries, marshes, sometimes large lakes FOOD Marine fish and invertebrates VOICE Nasal *nyeah*; distinctive *cow-cow-cow* call

KEY FACT The Mediterranean Gull is slightly larger and more robust than the similar-looking Black-headed Gull, has a sturdier, more colourful bill, and appears much whiter in flight as it lacks the Black-headed's dark wing markings.

IDENTIFICATION
Summer adults sport a black head with white 'eyelids', and a bright red bill with a yellow tip and dark sub-terminal band. Legs are red, back is pale grey, and body and underwings are white. Winter adults lose the black head, retaining only a smudged mask around eye. Juveniles retain dark markings on wings until their second winter.

STATUS AND HABITS
Once a rare bird in Britain, the Mediterranean Gull's breeding population has been slowly increasing since the 1950s. A hundred or so pairs now nest in the region, mostly in discrete colonies along the S coast of England. Birds frequently associate with flocks of Black-headed and Common gulls, and readily take to lingering around popular seaside holiday resorts in search of discarded picnic scraps.

SUMMER

LOCATION	DATE/TIME

WINTER

HERRING GULL
Larus argentatus

FACT FILE

SIZE Length 55–67cm **HABITAT** Coasts, city centres, large lakes, rivers, reservoirs **FOOD** Varied diet; often scavenges
VOICE Various staccato 'chuckling' calls and drawn-out *aahhooo* calls

IDENTIFICATION

Summer adults have a silvery-grey mantle, black wingtips with white flecks and an all-white underside. Bill is yellow with an orange spot near tip of lower mandible. Yellow eye has an orange eye-ring and legs are pink. Winter adults have brown speckles on head. Juveniles are mottled brown with a dark bill in their first year, gradually acquiring adult plumage over four years.

SUMMER

KEY FACT It is likely that Herring Gulls mate for life, and pairs have been known to return to the same nesting site for 20 years in succession.

LOCATION	DATE/TIME

STATUS AND HABITS

Herring Gulls are very adaptable, tough and resilient birds, able to exploit a wide range of habitats and food sources, and have learnt to find food in urban sites, open countryside, freshwater habitats, the coast and open seas. Scavenging provides much of their food, but they also prey on smaller birds, raiding nesting colonies and taking migrating birds. Showing little fear of humans, they respond to feeding opportunities in the centre of towns and readily nest on rooftops.

SUMMER

LESSER BLACK-BACKED GULL
Larus fuscus

FACT FILE

SIZE Length 55–60cm HABITAT Sea coasts; in winter, common on rubbish dumps, inland lakes and rivers
FOOD Omnivorous; scavenges fish and carrion VOICE Similar to that of Herring Gull but coarser and less screeching

IDENTIFICATION
Adult has a dark slate-grey back and upperwings and bright yellow legs, helping to distinguish it from the similar-looking Herring Gull. Underparts and head are white, and bill is yellow with a bright orange-red spot towards end of lower mandible. Juveniles remain in variable mottled grey-brown plumage, with a dark bill and flesh-coloured legs, until their third winter.

STATUS AND HABITS
Common around coastal habitats of the region, Lesser Black-backed Gulls are frequently seen loitering with large flocks of Herring Gulls. Adults

SUMMER

nest in colonies on well-vegetated coastal cliffs, high moors and islands, jointly defending the colony against any potential threats. They head S after breeding, but populations are bolstered by wintering birds from mainland Europe. Sizeable flocks are found around inland rubbish dumps, but coastal birds readily pluck shoaling fish from the surface and are even capable of taking small mammals and birds.

LOCATION	DATE/TIME

KEY FACT

The region's largest breeding colony of Lesser Black-backed Gulls is on Walney Island, Cumbria. The colony is suspected of harbouring over one-third of Britain's breeding population of 100,000-plus pairs.

WINTER

GREAT BLACK-BACKED GULL
Larus marinus

FACT FILE

SIZE **Length 65–78cm** HABITAT **Coastal, freshwater and urban habitats** FOOD **Omnivorous; takes animal prey and scavenges** VOICE **Typically gull-like; deep, gruff-sounding** *gaa-ga-ga* **call**

IDENTIFICATION

A bulky, powerful gull, the largest in the region. Adults are mostly black across back and upperwings, with a white head and underparts. Legs are flesh-coloured and bill is yellow with an orange spot. Juveniles do not acquire distinctive adult plumage until their fourth year, remaining scaly black-brown and developing a flesh-coloured bill with a black tip in their second year.

SUMMER

LOCATION	DATE/TIME

STATUS AND HABITS

Less numerous than other gull species, **Great Black-backs** are commonly encountered around the coasts of Britain throughout the breeding season. Almost 20,000 pairs breed in the region, nesting solitarily or in small colonies, usually on promontories close to larger seabird colonies. They are opportunistic feeders and will scavenge freely, snatch fish, eggs and chicks from other seabirds, and frequently take adult seabirds and Rabbits. In winter, they become more widespread inland, congregating at roosts on large lakes and reservoirs.

KEY FACT

Look closely at large mixed flocks of gulls. Great Black-backs are usually far less numerous, but their large size and very dark wings with a contrasting white border make them easy to spot, even at a distance.

SUMMER

GLAUCOUS GULL
Larus hyperboreus

FACT FILE

SIZE Length 65cm **HABITAT** Winter visitor to sheltered harbours, beaches, occasionally inland rubbish tips
FOOD Omnivorous scavenger **VOICE** Strained-sounding *kyaoo*, similar to a Herring Gull's call

IDENTIFICATION
Adults resemble adult Herring Gulls but are noticeably larger and stockier, and appear much paler because of their diagnostic white wingtips. Winter adults have buff-grey streaking on face, head and neck. Legs of all birds are pink. Juveniles have a pink bill with a black tip, and pale, mottled creamy-grey plumage that becomes streakier with age.

SUMMER

LOCATION	DATE/TIME

STATUS AND HABITS

A non-breeding winter visitor to the region from breeding grounds in the Arctic. Several hundred birds may turn up each year, mainly in coastal areas in N England and Scotland. Some non-breeding individuals will linger year-round. Glaucous Gulls are notorious scavengers, often found in sheltered fishing ports and harbours, where they scavenge fish waste and scraps discarded by boats. Solitary birds readily mingle with flocks of other large gull species, sometimes following them inland to lakes and rubbish tips.

SECOND SUMMER

KEY FACT

Glaucous Gulls have a slightly square head and small, pale eyes, giving them a somewhat menacing appearance. They use their size and bulk to steal food from other gulls.

ICELAND GULL
Larus glaucoides

FACT FILE

SIZE Length 52–60cm **HABITAT** Rare winter visitor to coasts; also inland reservoirs, landfill sites **FOOD** Mostly fish, fish scraps, carrion **VOICE** Typical gull-like calls and chattering, higher-pitched than Herring Gull

IDENTIFICATION
Closely resembles a Glaucous Gull in both juvenile and adult plumage, but is significantly smaller and less bulky, and wings appear longer and more pointed in flight. Neat, rounded head and daintier bill are said to give the gull a more 'pigeon-like' appearance. Legs of all birds are pink.

KEY FACT Despite their name, Iceland Gulls do not actually breed on Iceland. They nest singly or in small colonies on the coasts of Greenland and Arctic Canada.

WINTER

LOCATION	DATE/TIME

THIRD WINTER

STATUS AND HABITS

A rare winter visitor to Britain. Birds are most frequently found at coastal localities further N, particularly in the NW, but occasionally turn up at reservoir roosts or landfill sites inland. Usually fewer than 100 birds are recorded in the region each year. Solitary birds freely intermingle with flocks of other gull species. Wintering birds tend to linger around fishing harbours or other sources of readily available food until they are ready to return to their breeding grounds in the Arctic.

SANDWICH TERN
Sterna sandvicensis

SIZE Length 38–40cm **HABITAT** Mainly coastal, favouring sandy or gravelly shores and estuaries **FOOD** Fish – mainly smaller shoaling species **VOICE** Noisy around colonies; diagnostic loud, grating *kear-ick* flight call

IDENTIFICATION

An elegant, medium-sized seabird with long, narrow wings, a forked tail and a sharply pointed black bill with a yellow tip. Summer adults sport a smart black cap with a shaggy crest. Upperwings and back are pale grey, and body is white. Winter adults develop a white forehead. Juveniles are similar to winter adults but back is barred.

KEY FACT The Sandwich Tern was first described by the Kentish ornithologist John Latham in 1787. The name refers to the coastal town of Sandwich and Sandwich Bay in Kent.

LOCATION	DATE/TIME

STATUS AND HABITS

A summer visitor to the coasts of our region. Over 10,000 birds breed in scattered localities around Britain, with hotspots on the coasts of N Norfolk, Suffolk, Kent and the Solent. They nest in dense, noisy colonies on sandy beaches, often in association with other tern species. Most successful colonies exist on islands or in nature reserves where human disturbance can be minimised. Birds plunge-dive for fish, and small parties of birds will travel great distances from their colonies in search of food.

COMMON TERN
Sterna hirundo

FACT FILE

SIZE Length 31–35cm **HABITAT** Sheltered coasts, marshes, lakes, gravel pits **FOOD** Small fish, invertebrates **VOICE** Harsh, insistent *keey-yah* calls; various short alarm notes

IDENTIFICATION

Breeding adults have mostly pale grey upperparts, a black head, and a white tail, rump and underside. Short legs are bright red and bill is red with a dark tip. Primaries show dark tips, creating a dark wedge on outer wing in flight. Winter adults have a white forehead and mottled grey cap. Juveniles are similar to winter adults but with ginger mottling to upperparts and a paler orange black-tipped bill.

KEY FACT The very similar Arctic Tern has a shorter bill with no black on its tip, shorter red legs, and no dark patches on the primaries when seen in flight.

LOCATION	DATE/TIME

STATUS AND HABITS

Common Terns are elegant, slender-winged waterbirds with easy, buoyant flight, and are summer visitors to Britain from overwintering sites in tropical West Africa.

Nesting sites are usually shingle banks, sometimes away from water, and can be near coasts or well inland. They readily take to artificial floating platforms in reservoirs and gravel pits, and will travel considerable distances to fish. Colonial in habits, they will sometimes be found near Black-headed Gulls.

ARCTIC TERN
Sterna paradisaea

FACT FILE

SIZE Length 33–35cm HABITAT Mostly pelagic or coastal; sometimes on lakes and rivers on migration FOOD Fish, invertebrates VOICE Hard, chattering *krrt-krt-krt* alarm, called near nest

IDENTIFICATION

Resembles a Common Tern. Adults have a grey body, paler (appearing almost white) underparts, a black crown and long tail streamers. Uniformly blood-red bill and short red legs are diagnostic of the species. In flight and when viewed from below, wings appear pale, almost translucent, with a dark trailing edge to primaries. Juveniles have a scaly grey back, white underparts and an incomplete dark cap.

KEY FACT Arctic Terns undertake the longest regular migration of any bird species, with some individuals travelling over 20,000km from their feeding grounds in the Southern Ocean to their breeding colonies in the northern hemisphere.

LOCATION	DATE/TIME

STATUS AND HABITS

A summer visitor and passage migrant, breeding in isolated colonies, mostly on islands in the N of the region. Pairs mate for life, returning to the same colonies each year. They are particularly beautiful in flight, which is buoyant, appearing effortless, and they plunge-dive frequently for shoaling fish and marine invertebrates. The Arctic Tern is famous for its long annual migration to winter feeding grounds in the southern hemisphere. In our region, passage birds are commonly seen further S in spring and late summer, sometimes on inland lakes.

LITTLE TERN
Sterna albifrons

FACT FILE

SIZE Length 21–25cm **HABITAT** Shallow, sheltered coasts and estuaries; nests on sandy and shingle beaches **FOOD** Small fish, crustaceans **VOICE** Sharp, chattering *krret*

IDENTIFICATION

Britain's smallest tern. Summer adults have pure white underparts, grey upperwings and a grey back. Head sports a striking black cap and white forehead. Bill is distinctively yellow with a black tip, and legs are yellow-orange. Winter adults and juveniles have a whiter crown, and bill and legs are dark.

STATUS AND HABITS

A summer visitor that breeds in small, scattered colonies, mainly on the S and E coasts of Scotland and England. It is a strictly coastal species, nesting on sand and gravel beaches and foraging over relatively shallow water, often favouring marine lagoons, estuaries and saltmarsh creeks. The flight is buoyant, with birds hovering for prolonged periods and plunge-diving for small fish. Nesting colonies are very vulnerable to disturbance from humans and succeed only where human access is restricted. Birds begin to head S in Aug to their African wintering grounds.

LOCATION	DATE/TIME
- -	- - - - - - - - - - - -
- -	- - - - - - - - - - - -
- -	- - - - - - - - - - - -

KEY FACT

Little Terns often hunt for fish in very shallow water.
This can bring birds close to the shore, making it possible to observe
them at very close range as they hover and dive for fish.

PUFFIN
Fratercula arctica

SIZE Length 28–30cm **HABITAT** Mainly pelagic; nests in burrows on grassy cliff slopes **FOOD** Fish, especially sandeels **VOICE** Distinctive gargling *arrrh*, often repeated from within nest burrow

KEY FACT The Puffin's colourful bill is serrated to help it keep a firm grip on wriggling fish. Birds are capable of catching and holding dozens of sandeels before they return to the nest to feed their young.

IDENTIFICATION
Summer adults have a large, flattened bill marked with bright orange, blue and yellow, and black and red eye markings that contrast with dusky white cheeks. Upper body and neck are black, and underparts are white. Short legs and large, webbed feet are orange. Winter adults and juveniles have dusky grey faces, and the bill is smaller and duller.

LOCATION	DATE/TIME

STATUS AND HABITS

Instantly recognisable, Puffins are widely considered to be one of the most endearing seabirds in Britain. They spend much of their lives at sea and are strong swimmers, both on and below the water surface, capable of making deep dives in pursuit of fish. Adults come to shore only to breed, arriving at nesting colonies between Mar and Apr, when they nest in burrows excavated into grassy cliff slopes. Tens of thousands of birds nest at colonies on Skomer, the Farne Islands, Orkney and Shetland.

RAZORBILL
Alca torda

FACT FILE

SIZE Length 38–40cm HABITAT Mainly pelagic;
nests on coastal cliffs and boulder slopes FOOD Fish, mainly small
to medium-sized shoaling species VOICE Generally silent, but nesting
birds utter a deep croaking

IDENTIFICATION

A stocky black and white seabird. At close range, ridges and white lines can be seen on its distinctive flattened, blunt bill. Summer adults sport a sleek black head and upper body, and thin white wingbar. Underparts are white. Winter adults and juveniles have a whiter throat and cheeks, and a smaller bill.

STATUS AND HABITS

Birds are commonly seen on the coast during the breeding season but are rather scarce in inshore waters at other times. Most birds winter in the North Atlantic, but individuals are occasionally seen from seawatching points all year round. They swim well, dive frequently and often fly low over the water with distinctive whirring wingbeats. Razorbills favour rocky shores, mostly in the N and W of Britain, and nest amidst boulders and ledges on cliffs. They are often found alongside similar seabirds but are far less numerous than guillemots and Puffins.

LOCATION	DATE/TIME

KEY FACT

Razorbills do not construct nests, laying their large, robust eggs directly onto bare rock. The eggs are uniquely speckled, enabling parents to identify their own clutch easily in the mêlée of a busy colony.

GUILLEMOT
Uria aalge

SIZE Length 40cm **HABITAT** Pelagic; nests on steep coastal cliffs **FOOD** Fish **VOICE** Nasal growling and chattering around nesting cliffs

FACT FILE

IDENTIFICATION

Summer adults have a dark, matt brown head and upperparts, and bright white underparts. Bill is dark, straight and dagger-like. So-called 'bridled' Guillemots sport fine white 'spectacle' marks around eyes. Winter adults become whiter on face, particularly around cheeks and throat. Juveniles resemble winter adults.

STATUS AND HABITS

In summer, over a million Guillemots congregate around localised colonies in Britain, mainly along rocky N and W coastlines. They are typically the most numerous species at many seabird colonies, usually crammed together on tiny ledges over the most precipitous cliffs. Outside of the breeding season they spend most of their time at sea and are rarely seen in inshore waters. They are excellent swimmers and use their wings and feet to dive to depths of 60m in pursuit of fish.

LOCATION	DATE/TIME

KEY FACT

Guillemots lay their eggs directly onto narrow cliff ledges. The eggs are distinctly conical, which prevents them from rolling off the ledges and into the sea.

BRIDLED FORM

BLACK GUILLEMOT
Cepphus grille

SIZE Length 31–33cm **HABITAT** Inshore and pelagic waters on rocky coasts **FOOD** Mostly fish and marine crustaceans **VOICE** High-pitched whistle, descending in tone

IDENTIFICATION

Smaller and more elegant than the robust Guillemot. Summer adults have dark brown (almost black) plumage, with bright white patches on wings. Feet and gape are bright red. Winter adults appear mainly white, with grey barring on head, neck and mantle. They retain a black tail and the distinctive black wings with white wing patches. Juveniles resemble winter adults, but head, breast and rump are dusky, and distinct barring on white wing patch remains until second summer.

LOCATION	DATE/TIME

STATUS AND HABITS

Birds breed on the rocky coastlines of Ireland and N and W coasts of Scotland; Shetland and Orkney are strongholds. They nest solitarily or in small, scattered colonies. Nest sites are well hidden amidst the cracks and crevices of boulder slopes, or sometimes in holes on harbour walls and jetties. Resident birds are fairly sedentary, remaining in inshore waters for most of the year, where they dive in search of bottom-dwelling fish and crustaceans.

LITTLE AUK
Alle alle

SIZE Length 18–19cm **HABITAT** Pelagic
FOOD Mostly planktonic crustaceans
VOICE Silent in the region

IDENTIFICATION

A tiny auk with a stubby black bill. Winter adults have a black cap, nape and back, with a white throat and underparts. White lines on upperwing are visible when viewed at close range. Summer adults and juveniles are never seen in Britain.

LOCATION	DATE/TIME

KEY FACT

Late autumn is usually the best time to look for Little Auks. For the best chances of seeing them, visit popular seawatching points along the E coast of England and Scotland.

STATUS AND HABITS

A winter visitor to Britain's offshore waters from its breeding grounds on Arctic cliffs. Most birds winter in the North Atlantic, where they dive in search of pelagic zooplankton and small fish. They rarely venture close to shore, but feeding flocks are thought to move into the North Sea in search of food and strong onshore gales sometimes blow large numbers of birds within sight of land. Even at a distance, their tiny size and rapid, whirring wingbeats are quite distinctive.

SHORELARK
Eremophila alpestris

FACT FILE

SIZE Length 16–18cm **HABITAT** Winter visitor on open shores **FOOD** Seeds, insects
VOICE Thin *see-seer* flight call

IDENTIFICATION

Summer adults are quite distinctive, with a yellow face adorned with a broad black breast-band, a black stripe through eye and ear coverts, and black feather tufts ('horns') on head. Upperparts are sandy brown, streaky on back, and underparts are white with buff streaks on flanks. Winter adults are duller and lack the distinctive 'horns'. Juveniles resemble winter adults but have spangled upperparts and more barring on breast and flanks.

LOCATION	DATE/TIME

STATUS AND HABITS

Essentially a scarce winter visitor from its Scandinavian breeding grounds to the exposed, open shores of the E coast of England. The numbers of birds that winter in the region each year is highly variable, ranging from several hundred to just a few dozen individuals. Birds remain almost exclusively coastal during their stay and are often seen foraging in small flocks along the margins of dry fields, dune slacks and saltmarshes. They are quite unobtrusive when feeding in long vegetation and can be difficult to spot.

KEY FACT

When in summer plumage, the Shorelark's head tufts are so distinctive that in North America (and increasingly in parts of Europe) the bird is commonly known as the Horned Lark.

WINTER

SKYLARK
Alauda arvensis

FACT FILE

SIZE Length 18cm **HABITAT** Open countryside;
common on coastal grasslands, moorlands, dunes
FOOD Seeds, insects **VOICE** Continuous, rapid, chirping,
trilling, sometimes mimetic song; sharp, rolling *churrrp* call

IDENTIFICATION

A large but rather inconspicuous, streaky sandy-brown lark. Adults have a
buff breast with dark streaks; underparts are paler. Head has a short but
distinctive crest that is raised when birds are excited or alarmed. White
outer-tail feathers and pale trailing edge to wings are obvious in flight.
Juveniles are similar to adults but have a more scaly appearance.

LOCATION	DATE/TIME

KEY FACT
Birds are famed for their hovering display flight and joyous, frolicking song, which for many years has provided inspiration for numerous songwriters and poets.

STATUS AND HABITS
A widespread breeding bird of open grassy habitats throughout the region; common on coastal grasslands in winter, when resident populations are boosted by migrants from Scandinavia. They typically favour areas of low, dry vegetation, where their streaky plumage affords them good camouflage as they forage for insects and seeds. Sky Larks are reluctant to fly when disturbed, instead often choosing to run or crouch in cover. The species' breeding success is inextricably linked to changes in farming practices, and populations have undergone drastic declines in recent decades.

MEADOW PIPIT
Anthus pratensis

FACT FILE

SIZE Length 14.5cm HABITAT Open grasslands, bogs, marshes FOOD Mostly invertebrates; some seeds in winter VOICE Quiet *tsip* calls; whistling flight calls

IDENTIFICATION

Adults have mostly olive-brown upperparts, grading into darker buff-brown with darker streaks on crown and back. Rump is brighter olive-brown. Underparts are greyish white with olive tinges, and a chest-band of dark spots and streaks extends onto flanks. Legs are pinkish buff and bill is grey-brown. Juveniles have heavier streaking on upperparts and clearer pale margins on wing feathers.

LOCATION	DATE/TIME

KEY FACT The Meadow
Pipit sings in flight, starting from
a high point and 'parachuting'
down while delivering its short,
melodious song, which ends in
a descending scale.

STATUS AND HABITS

Meadow Pipits are widespread and
common in suitable habitats, but
are easily overlooked owing to their coloration, which helps them blend
perfectly with grassland vegetation. If alarmed, they fly off quickly and
dive into cover, giving their characteristic *tsip* calls. Neatly constructed
grassy nests lined with hair are hidden in dense vegetation, the only clue
to breeding birds being the spring song and display flight. In winter, they
may mix with other pipits to feed on strand-lines, on the edge of lakes and
on marshes.

ROCK PIPIT
Anthus petrosus

SIZE Length 16cm **HABITAT** Rocky shores
FOOD Small invertebrates **VOICE** Explosive series of descending, jangling notes uttered during display flight; sharp *pseet* call

IDENTIFICATION

A rather stocky, drab grey bird, larger than a Meadow Pipit. Upperparts are streaky grey-brown, pale underparts are off-white, and breast and flanks are heavily streaked. A rather indistinct, pale supercilium and eye-ring are sometimes visible. Throat is pale with a dark sub-moustachial stripe.

LOCATION	DATE/TIME

KEY FACT Rock Pipits look very similar to their more strikingly marked cousin the Water Pipit. For many years these birds were considered to be the same species.

STATUS AND HABITS

Rock Pipits are a strictly coastal species, present on rocky shores throughout the region. During the breeding season they are most common on N and W coasts, where they nest around rocky cliff slopes.

Their distinctive parachuting display flight starts from high rocky outcrops and usually terminates on a prominent boulder at a lower level. Outside of the breeding season the birds become more widespread; at this time they are more frequently found foraging on beaches and strand-lines in the S and E of the region.

PIED WAGTAIL
Motacilla alba yarellii

FACT FILE

SIZE **Length 18cm** HABITAT **Mainly near water;
some urban sites** FOOD **Small invertebrates**
VOICE **Loud** *chizzick* **contact notes; rapid warbling, twittering song**

IDENTIFICATION

Breeding male has black on crown, nape, chin and upper breast. Upperparts
are mostly black but with white fringes to wing feathers and outer-tail
feathers. Breeding female is similar but with a greyer back. Non-breeding
adults lack black throat. Juveniles are similar to non-breeding female but
with a browner tinge to plumage and buff fringes on larger wing feathers.

WINTER MALE

LOCATION	DATE/TIME

KEY FACT

At night Pied Wagtails often gather in large flocks for communal roosting, favouring sheltered reedbeds, sewage plants or even town centre buildings where there may be some warmth.

STATUS AND HABITS

This is the British and Irish subspecies of the White Wagtail, a very widespread bird across Continental Europe. Active and lively, Pied Wagtails are easily spotted as they feed on insects, sometimes making short dashes along the ground to catch them. Their swooping flight and frequent calls also draw attention. They prefer to feed in open habitats where insects are plentiful, and can be found in city parks and urban sites as well as beside water. Nests are built in natural or artificial crevices.

SUMMER

JACKDAW
Corvus monedula

FACT FILE

SIZE **Length 31–34cm** HABITAT **Open countryside,
towns and coasts** FOOD **Invertebrates, fruit, seeds; will scavenge
scraps and carrion** VOICE **Short, nasal** *chack*

IDENTIFICATION

A relatively small member of the crow family. Adults have a distinguished
silver-grey nape and piercing grey eyes. Rest of plumage is mainly glossy
black, darkest on crown and wings. Juveniles frequently appear less glossy
and more brown, and eye is duller.

KEY FACT Jackdaws construct large twiggy nests inside holes in
trees, on cliffs or even in chimneys. Fresh twigs are added to popular
nest sites each year – large nests can contain over 25kg of sticks.

LOCATION	DATE/TIME

STATUS AND HABITS

A widespread and common breeding bird throughout most of the region, although the species is largely absent from the Highlands of Scotland. Intelligent and adaptable, Jackdaws are equally at home foraging for seeds and insects in cultivated fields as they are searching for dead fish and crabs along winter strand-lines. They readily take carrion, and often linger around car parks and picnic sites in search of scraps. This highly gregarious species nests in noisy colonies and is frequently seen flying in large, acrobatic flocks.

CHOUGH
Pyrrhocorax pyrrhocorax

FACT FILE

SIZE Length 38–40cm **HABITAT** Coastal cliffs with short grassland and caves **FOOD** Soil invertebrates; some seeds and berries taken in winter **VOICE** High-pitched, nasal *chiaa*

IDENTIFICATION

Adults sport a long, downcurved, bright red bill and similarly coloured legs and feet. Plumage is glossy black. Juveniles are very similar but legs are duller and bill is a pale yellow. Choughs are fairly obvious in flight: highly vocal and acrobatic, with noticeably broad wings and 'fingered' wingtips.

STATUS AND HABITS

A scarce resident in the region. A few hundred pairs breed, but only on coastal cliffs that provide both short grassland and a selection of caves and crevices suitable for nesting. Distribution is restricted mainly to W coasts of Ireland and Wales, the Isle of Man and a few of the Hebridean islands. Birds use their scimitar-like bill to probe coastal pastures for subterranean insects. In winter, they form large flocks and frequently feed along strand-lines.

LOCATION	DATE/TIME

KEY FACT

Chough populations have been badly affected by changing agricultural practices, but in recent years they have started to make a comeback, and have successfully recolonised some of their former haunts on the rocky coasts of Cornwall.

RAVEN
Corvus corax

SIZE Length 55–65cm **HABITAT** Coastal cliffs, mountains, wooded hillsides **FOOD** Mainly carrion; generally omnivorous **VOICE** Deep, loud *cronk* call

IDENTIFICATION
The largest member of the crow family and the largest passerine in the region. Plumage is jet black and, when seen in good light, has an oily, iridescent sheen. Bill is huge and powerful, neck is thick and throat is shaggy. In flight, wedge-shaped tail is an obvious diagnostic feature.

LOCATION	DATE/TIME

KEY FACT

Observations have shown that Ravens have remarkable problem-solving abilities, and the birds are thought to be highly intelligent. Years of persecution by gamekeepers and landowners have made them remarkably wary of humans.

STATUS AND HABITS

A resident species with a distinct **W** distribution in the region. Nesting birds favour rather remote, isolated headlands and rocky outcrops but forage widely in a range of habitats. They are opportunistic scavengers, feeding on a variety of plant and animal material, but their large size and powerful build makes them effective predators capable of taking seabirds and Rabbits. Young birds tend to form small flocks, but mated pairs defend territories and spend much of their lives together.

CARRION CROW
Corvus corone

SIZE Length 45–50cm HABITAT Everywhere, from seashores to cities FOOD Omnivorous; mainly scavengers VOICE Harsh, croaking *kraaa-kraaa-craaa*

IDENTIFICATION

The archetype by which all other corvids are compared. Carrion Crows are fairly large and robust, with uniformly black plumage. They have a stout bill and black legs. They are far less gregarious than either Rooks or Jackdaws, and are usually seen only singly or in pairs.

LOCATION	DATE/TIME

STATUS AND HABITS

A common resident species with a widespread distribution throughout England and Wales, extending into the S and E of Scotland. Carrion Crows are clever and adaptable, able to exploit a wide variety of habitats. They take carrion, scavenge scraps from landfill sites and even feed off garden bird tables. Many coastal populations have learned to open shellfish: some drop them onto rocks from a height, some use stones to strike them, and others place them in the road and allow traffic to do the work.

KEY FACT

Carrion Crows are cautious of humans but quickly learn to exploit any food source. They commonly linger in the vicinity of busy car parks, picnic sites and duck ponds in the hope of scoring an easy meal.

HOODED CROW
Corvus cornix

SIZE Length 45–50cm **HABITAT** Coastal shores, moorland, mountains **FOOD** Omnivorous; mainly scavengers **VOICE** Harsh, croaking *kraaa-kraaa-craaa*

IDENTIFICATION

Identical in size and shape to the Carrion Crow, but with striking bicoloured plumage consisting of a black head and bib (similar to an executioner's hood), black wings and tail, and a distinctive ashy-grey 'waistcoat'.

LOCATION	DATE/TIME

STATUS AND HABITS

Hooded Crows are similar to Carrion Crows in all respects, and are equally resourceful and intelligent. Their distribution is limited within the region, being restricted primarily to NW Scotland (N of an imaginary line between the Firth of Clyde and the Dornoch Firth) and Ireland. There is little overlap with the Carrion Crow apart from on the Isle of Man, where that species dominates. Vagrant birds from Scandinavia occasionally appear along the E coast of England and sometimes stay for many years.

KEY FACT

An estimated 200,000 pairs of Hooded Crows breed within the region. Despite the species' restricted range, it is therefore still a common British breeding bird.

LINNET
Carduelis cannabina

SIZE Length 14cm **HABITAT** Lowland open country, waysides, hedgerows **FOOD** Seeds **VOICE** Slightly nasal, twittering *tetter-tett*

FACT FILE

IDENTIFICATION

Summer males has a chestnut-brown back, grey head and striking rosy-red forehead. Underparts are paler buff and breast is flushed red. Winter male loses red markings. Female and juveniles appear grey-brown with pale underparts and a heavily streaked breast. Small, triangular bill is grey in both sexes at all times.

JUVENILE

LOCATION	DATE/TIME
- -	- - - - - - - - - -
- -	- - - - - - - - - -
- -	- - - - - - - - - -
- -	- - - - - - - - - -

STATUS AND HABITS

A year-round resident that is widespread throughout the region but scarce in upland areas. It is particularly common on the E coast. Breeding birds nest in gorse thickets, hedgerows and scrub, and typically feed in open arable fields and meadows. They take a variety of small 'weed' seeds and are dependent on these being available throughout the year; changes in farming have taken their toll on many populations. Many birds move closer to the coasts in winter, where they feed in coastal fields and saltmarshes.

KEY FACT

Linnets form large, twittering winter flocks that are often heard before they are seen. They were once a very popular cagebird because of their bright colours and melodious song.

TWITE
Carduelis flavirostris

FACT FILE

SIZE Length 14cm **HABITAT** Breeds on maritime and
mountain moorlands; winters on saltmarshes and coastal fields
FOOD Seeds **VOICE** Sharp *tveeht* call; song is typically a series of fast
trilling and twittering notes

IDENTIFICATION

A dumpy, heavily streaked cousin of the similar-looking Linnet. Breeding
male is tawny brown with dark streaking on back and breast, pale
underparts and a pink rump. Face and throat are unstreaked, appearing
buff, and bill is grey. Breeding female and juvenile resemble breeding male
but with a brown rump. In all birds bill is grey in summer and yellow in
winter, when markings are more subdued.

SUMMER MALE

LOCATION	DATE/TIME

JUVENILE

KEY FACT The coasts of East Anglia generally prove to be the best place to look for Twite in winter. Flocks are commonly found on the saltmarshes on the N Norfolk coast.

STATUS AND HABITS

A resident breeding species, with approximately 10,000 birds breeding on remote upland and coastal moorlands of N England, Wales and the Highlands and Islands of Scotland. They typically favour areas where traditional crofting-type agriculture is still employed and an abundance of small seeds can be found. In winter, birds move nearer to the coast, feeding on saltmarshes and coastal fields. Winter populations are bolstered by birds from N Europe, when their range extends dramatically S, particularly along the E coast.

SNOW BUNTING
Plectrophenax nivalis

FACT FILE

SIZE Length 16–18cm HABITAT Breeds in Arctic and rocky alpine zones; winters on short coastal grasslands, dunes and saltmarshes; FOOD Seeds, insects VOICE Tinkling song; distinctive, rippling *prr-r-r-it*

IDENTIFICATION

A large, plump bunting with white wing panels and white on rump and tail. Summer male appears very white, with a black back, bill and legs. Summer female is similar but streakier brown and buff on back, and with buff around head and neck. Winter adults have mainly white underparts and buff-orange upperparts; bill is yellow. Juveniles have a grey head and mottled breast, and lack the adults' white wing panels.

KEY FACT Snow Buntings are often quite confiding. They happily feed on grasslands around busy seaside cafés and car parks, and some even take to scrounging scraps from picnic tables.

WINTER MALE

LOCATION	DATE/TIME

STATUS AND HABITS

Snow Buntings are a rare breeding
species in the region, with fewer than
100 pairs nesting within the restricted
rocky alpine zones of the Scottish
Highlands. They are rarely seen
outside of this range during the
breeding season, and are more
familiar as a winter visitor from
their breeding grounds in Scandinavia.
Up to 10,000 birds descend on the
E coasts of England and Scotland
every year from mid-Sep onwards,
sometimes congregating in flocks
on the grassy margins of windswept
beaches, dune slacks and saltmarshes.

FIRST WINTER

LAPLAND BUNTING
Calcarius lapponicus

FACT FILE

SIZE Length 14–16cm **HABITAT** Breeds on wet mountain moors, tundra scrub; winters on coastal fields and saltmarshes **FOOD** Seeds **VOICE** Short, whistled *tchu*; distinctive dry, rattling *pr'r'r'rt* in flight

IDENTIFICATION

Summer adults are rarely seen in the region. Winter adults and juveniles have a dark speckled bib, a dark brown crown, a reddish-brown face and a dark (almost black) line defining ear coverts. Back is reddish brown and heavily streaked, often showing two pale wingbars. Underparts are pale with streaked flanks.

WINTER MALE

LOCATION	DATE/TIME

STATUS AND HABITS

A scarce (only a few hundred birds each year) winter visitor to the
E coast, usually ranging from Kent to SE Scotland. Passage birds are
occasionally seen in Scotland in summer, when males sport striking black and white plumage around their head and breast. During their stay, wintering birds rarely leave the coast, spending much of their time on the ground foraging for seeds. They readily mingle with flocks of other buntings, larks and finches.

KEY FACT Lapland Buntings can be a difficult bird to spot. They are generally very wary and frequently take flight at the slightest disturbance. Solitary birds are the easiest to approach.

JUVENILE

Common names are in plain text and scientific names are in *italic*.

PHOTOGRAPHIC ACKNOWLEDGEMENTS

Photographs supplied by Nature Photographers Ltd. All photographs by Paul Sterry except for the those on the following pages:

Laurie Campbell: 40; Andrew Cleave: 140, 161; Ernie Janes: 82, 95, 107; Owen Newman: 70; David Osborn: 61; Richard Revels: 66, 144–5, 153, 155, 157; EK Thompson: 146; Roger Tidman: 67, 109, 125, 170, 176.